circuit hikes

in
virginia, west virginia,
maryland, and pennsylvania

potomac appalachian trail club
washington, d.c.
1986

Guide to Circuit Hikes
In Virginia, West Virginia, Maryland and Pennsylvania

Text by
Jean Golightly

Maps by
Lynn T. Gallagher
K.C. Kraft
Jean Golightly

Photos by
Jean Golightly

1986
Fourth Edition
POTOMAC APPALACHIAN TRAIL CLUB
1718 N Street, N.W.
Washington, D.C. 20036

Library of Congress Catalog Number 85-060393

ISBN NO. 0-915746-29-8

Copyright © 1986 by the Potomac Appalachian Trail Club
1718 N Street, N.W.
Washington, D.C. 20036

PATC CIRCUIT HIKES

Introduction v

Hike No. Name	mi	km	page
Northern Virginia			
1. Burke Lake Park	5.9	9.5	1
2. Manassas Battlefield Park	5.3	8.5	5
3. Dranesville District Park	3.2	5.2	9
4. Difficult Run	5.0	8.0	13
5. Prince Wm. Forest-Pyrite Mine Loop	6.0	9.7	17
6. Prince Wm. Forest-Beaver Loop	11.5	18.5	19
Massanutten Mountain			
7. Signal Knob	9.8	15.8	23
8. Duncan Knob	7.5	12.1	25
9. Bird Knob	8.5	13.7	29
Great North Mountain-Wolf Gap Area			
10. Big Schloss	12.0	19.3	33
11. Pond Run-Half-Moon Lookout	10.5	16.9	37
12. Little Sluice Mtn.-White Rock Cliff	14.2	22.9	39
13. Big Blue-Cove Run	9.0	14.5	45
14. Laurel Run-Stack Rock	8.2	13.2	49
Maryland			
15. Billy Goat Trail	4.0	6.4	51
16. Great Falls	3.7	6.0	55
17. Maryland Heights-Buggy Rock	4.6	7.4	57
	or		
	9.8	15.8	
18. Sugar Loaf Mountain	7.1	11.4	61
	or	71	
	8.1	13.0	
19. Wolf-Chimney Rocks	8.7	14.0	67
20. Cat Rock	4.4	7.1	71
Pennsylvania-Michaux State Forest			
21. Caledonia-Quarry Gap	7.4	11.9	73
22. Tumbling Run-Lewis Rocks	5.0	8.1	77
23. Sunset Rocks	4.8	7.7	81
24. Pole Steeple	6.3	10.1	83
25. Rocky Knob	4.2	6.8	87

**The Potomac Apalachian Trail Club
1718 N Street, N.W.
Washington, D.C. 20036
Telephone 202/638-5306**

This GUIDE is published by the Potomac Appalachian Trail Club. The Club is a volunteer group whose main purpose is the preservation and maintenance of a section of the Appalachian Trail, part of which is covered herein. The Club is also responsible for a variety of maps, other publications, hiking and climbing, ski-touring excursions, and other activities. The Club Headquarters is open week-day evenings from 7 p.m. to 10 p.m. except holidays. Visitors and callers are welcome.

In a Guide such as this it is inevitable that errors, both typographical and factual, will occur. Please report any you find to the editor, in care of PATC, so that they may be corrected in future editions.

The Potomac Appalachian Trail Club expressly denies any liability for any accident or injury to persons using these trails.

Introduction

When the idea for this book was first suggested to me, I—like most of you—had done all of my local hiking in the Shenandoah National Park. When I think back I wonder how I could have been naive enough to think that one section of mountains with "park boundary" marked on its edges was the only place worth hiking. The past 2½ years have been a truly exciting experience "discovering" and exploring all of these other lovely places filled with flowers, clear cool streams, waterfalls, rocks, cliffs, overlooks and wildlife. THEY'RE NOT ALL IN THE SHENANDOAH! And most hikes are no further away than the southern section of the park, many are closer. Most are in the George Washington National Forest, a few are in state and regional parks, a few in state forest and one is on private land. Some are flat, others rugged; some can be done in an afternoon, others will be a rough all day trip; some offer mountaintop views, in others the interest is within the forest itself. Read the introductions then pick the one that suits your mood and time schedule—and enjoy them as much as I have.

Jean Golightly

Tips for Hikers

Total Travel Distance—This is the distance as measured from the first intersection mentioned, usually the point at which you leave I-495.

Trail Signs—They appear and disappear from time to time. Keep track of your whereabouts on the map and don't depend on the signs.

Maps—Although the maps in this book are sufficient for finding your way, the PATC and USGS maps will provide a better overall picture of the area or more detail.

Time—Allow ample time to return to your car before dark. Consider not only the length of the hike but also the elevation gain. An average estimate is 30 minutes per mile plus 30 minutes for each 1,000 feet of elevation gain. (This does not include lunch stops, sunbathing or footsoaking stops.) Know what time the sun sets, especially if hiking in winter.

Itinerary—Leave your route with someone at home, also expected time of return. Hike with a companion.

Weather—In the mountains weather can change rapidly. Carry a raincoat, extra sweater, extra food. Be familiar with the symptoms and treatment of hypothermia.

Litter—Nobody enjoys hiking on a messy trail. Be sure to carry out everything you carry in.

Poisonous Snakes—Rattlesnakes and copperheads may be found in the areas of most of these hikes. They are not aggressive but will not take kindly to being stepped upon. Watch where you walk and where you put your hands, especially when climbing rocks.

Hunting Season—Many of these hikes are in areas open for hunting. In general, deer season runs from mid November to early January. Check specific state and county regulations.

Four Hikes in One—Expand your hiking experiences to include all four seasons. Each has its own rewards.

LEGEND

TRAIL BLAZES

Single blazes mark the trail

Double blazes means "watch for a change of direction"

ROADS

──────── First and Second Grade Roads (paved)

──────── Third and Fourth Grade Roads (gravel or dirt)

TRAILS

················· Appalachian Trail

—·—·—·— Other trail

— — — — Forest road

SYMBOLS

★ Start of Hike
┼ Gate
○ Wildlife Clearing
■ Building
π Shelter
♀ Spring

ABBREVIATIONS

All maps drawn to 100 foot contour intervals. Because of the limited elevation change, no contour lines appear on maps No. 1 and No. 2.

AT	Appalachian Trail	**PATC**	Potomac Appalachian Trail Club
km.	kilometer		
mi.	mile	**USGS**	United States Geological Survey

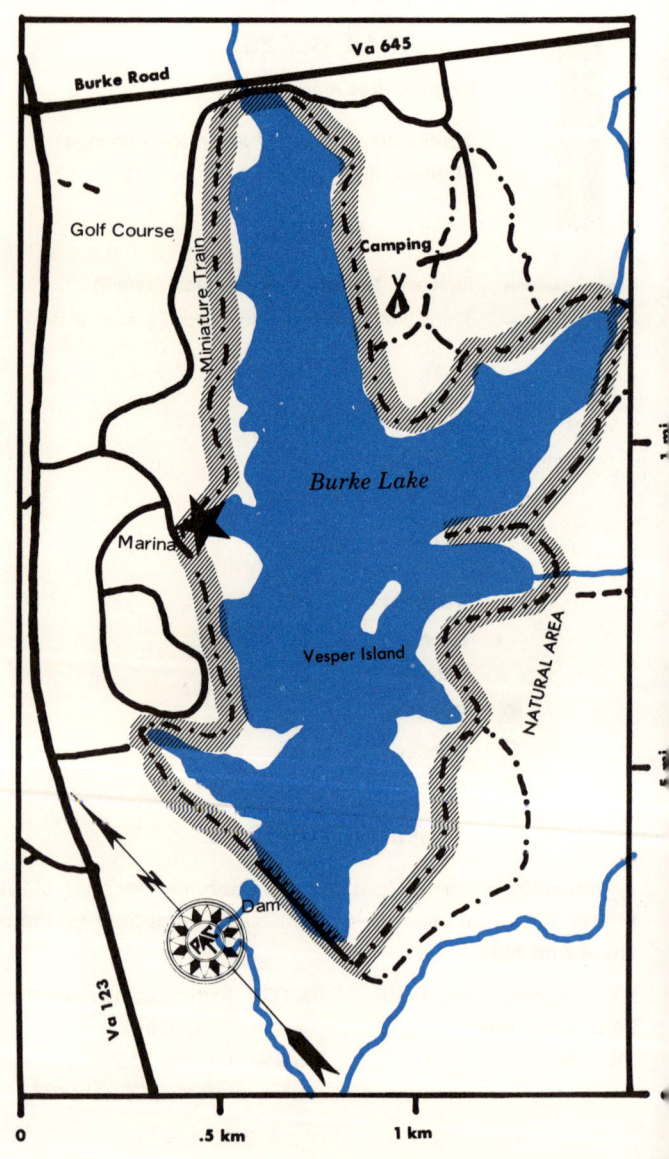

Hike No. 1

1 Burke Lake Park
Fairfax County, Virginia

Length: 5.9 mi. (9.5 km.)
Elevation Change: None.
Sketch map available at Visitor Center.
USGS Quad: Fairfax, Va.

This is a flat, woodland trail which follows the jagged contours of Burke Lake. Distance may vary somewhat depending on how closely the lake edge is followed. The hike begins at the marina, then crosses the dam and passes through an area which has been designated as a natural area, harboring a variety of wildlife including beavers, red fox, grey fox, white-tailed deer and mink. After passing Vesper Island, a wildlife sanctuary, the trail rounds the end of the lake, passing the camping area, nature trail and miniature train before returning to the marina.

Although likely to be crowded in summer and warm weekends, this is a delightful walk in winter and on weekdays. The lake is a wintering spot for numerous species of waterfowl such as buffleheads, coots, mallards, muscovies and Canada geese, with the usual array of wildflowers in the spring.

Travel Directions: I-495 to I-66; I-66 west to Va 123; Va 123 south about 9 miles (14.5 km.) to park entrance on left, just beyond golf course. Follow signs to marina and park in lot. (A parking fee is charged for non-residents of Fairfax County.)

Total Travel Distance: 13 mi. (22 km.).

Trail Data

km.	mi.	
0.0	0.0	Marina; bear right along edge of lake.
1.4	0.9	Apex of inlet; join bike trail.
1.9	1.2	Dam; cross dam on wide trail, then stay left on narrow trail or continue on wide bike trail.

3.4	**2.1**	Rejoin bike trail.
4.4	**2.7**	Side trail to left leads out to narrow point of land.
4.7	**2.9**	Return to main trail and turn left.
7.7	**4.8**	Road; bear left along lake edge; pass miniature train.
9.5	**5.9**	Marina.

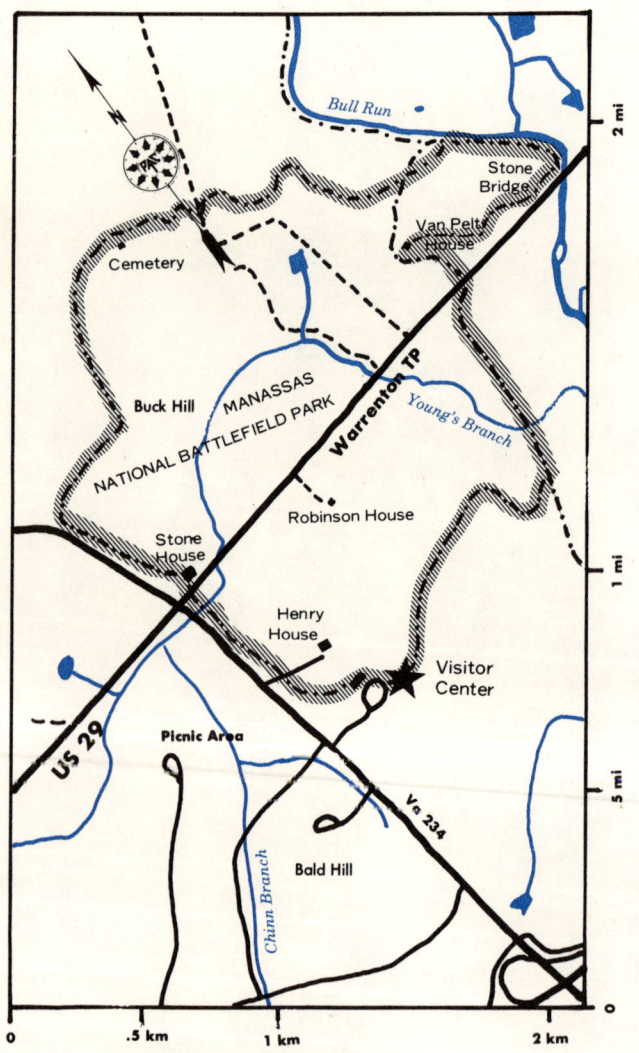

Hike No. 2
2 Manassas Battlefield Park
Manassas, Virginia

Length: 5.2 mi. (8.4 km.)
Elevation Change: Minimal.
Map available at Visitor Center.
USGS Quad: Gainesville, Va.

Manassas Battlefield park contains about 20 miles of hiking trails which follow the campaign routes of such Generals as Beauregard, Evans, Jackson, Pope and McClellan in the Civil War battles of First and Second Manassas. For those wishing a more complete historical background, there is an excellent slide program shown in the Visitor Center, also a map and brochure describing points of interest and progress of the battles along the way.

The circuit described below includes paths through open fields, along the woods edge and through the woods along Bull Run. It passes Old Stone Bridge, site of the first shots fired in battle in 1861. Further on the trail leads to the Old Stone House, General Pope's headquarters and later a Union field hospital, leading finally to the Visitor Center once again.

Travel Directions: I-495 to I-66; I-66 west to Va 234 at Manassas; Va 234 north (right) to park entrance on right.

Total Travel Distance: 14 mi. (23 km.)

Trail Data

km. *mi.*

0.0 **0.0** Face Visitor Center and walk right, passing to right of Stonewall Jackson statue. Continue to angle right onto mowed path leading between cannons.

0.2 **0.1** Sign for First Manassas Trail and Van Pelt House Site. (Follow blue dots for most of hike.) Continue straight ahead, then bear right into woods on blue dot trail, leaving wide trail.

0.8 **0.5** Cross yellow-blazed bridle trail.

1.3 0.8 Cross bridle trail and immediately turn left onto woods road which runs parallel to it; cross Young's Branch.

1.9 1.2 Leave well worn road and bear left on blue dot trail; cross US 29 (Warrenton Turnpike). Follow mowed path along edge of field with row of trees to right.

2.3 1.4 Top of hill; walk right to site of Van Pelt House; turn right again, following blue dot trail which is now joined by white cloverleaf Loop Trail. Descend and follow boardwalk.

3.1 1.9 Parking lot and Old Stone Bridge. Just before bridge, turn left and follow trail along Bull Run.

3.7 2.3 Farm Ford; leave Loop Trail and turn left on blue dot trail toward cemetery.

4.0 2.5 Reach field and turn right along edge of woods.

4.2 2.6 Bridle trail goes right; a little beyond, take mowed path which cuts across field then continues along edge of woods.

5.0 3.1 Cross gravel road.

5.3 3.3 Carter House Site. To reach cemetery, follow trail to left for 80 yds., bearing right at fork. Return to main trail and turn left.

6.4 4.0 Cross bridle trail and shortly enter field with cannons on left.

6.8 4.2 Just before Va 234 (Manassas-Sudley Rd.), turn left on mowed path on inside of fence.

7.6 4.7 Old Stone House; cross US 29; cross small bridge on Va 234 then bear left to mowed path inside fence.

7.9 4.9 A lone cedar tree marks top of ridge; follow mowed path along fence, then turn left onto driveway; Henry House is on left, Visitor Center to right.

8.4 5.2 Visitor Center.

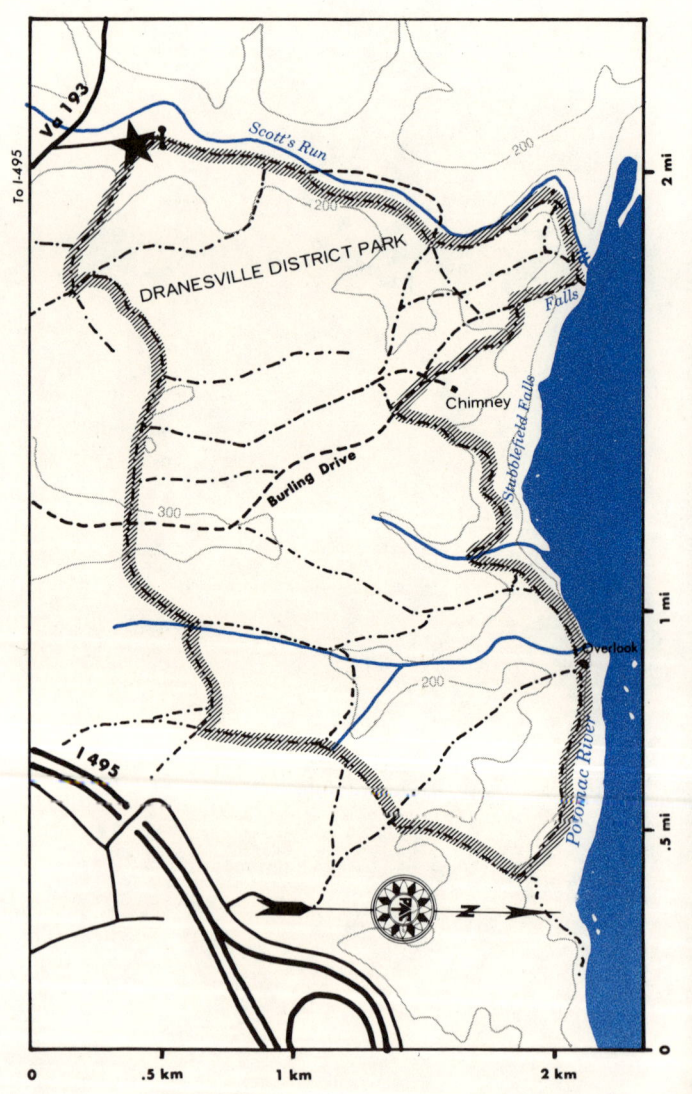

Hike No. 3
3 Dranesville District Park
Dranesville, Virginia

Length: 3.2 mi. (5.2 km.)
Elevation Change: Minimal.
PATC Map D.
USGS Quad: Falls Church, Va.

This 335 acre park, formerly known as the Burling Tract, was the scene of much controversy a few years ago when threatened with a housing development. The route described here covers mostly gentle terrain, except for one spot which requires a little rock scramble. The trail first follows Scott's Run which is lined with tall hemlocks, then emerges from the woods beside a waterfall as the stream tumbles into the Potomac. Next the trail passes the site of the old homestead with only its chimney still standing, then branches off onto a narrow, little traveled path which skirts the bluffs above the Potomac, offering several good overlooks. The sounds of the rapids of Stubblefield Falls gradually give way to the sounds of the traffic on the beltway as you return through the woods to the parking area.

This park is honey-combed with trails, offering many miles of hiking over gently rolling terrain, along Scott's Run and along the Potomac. Some of the major trails are described in this circuit, but don't hesitate to explore the others. Since the park is bounded by Scott's Run, the Potomac, the Beltway and Va 193, it is unlikely that you would stay lost for any considerable time.

Travel Directions: I-495 to Va 193; Va 193 west 0.6 mi. (1.0 km.) to parking lot on right with sign, just before small bridge. Parking area is not visible until you are in front of it, so drive slowly.

Total Travel Distance: 0.6 m. (1.0 km.)

Trail Data

km.   *mi.*

0.0   **0.0**   Walk to rear of parking lot, pass gate and follow old road beside Scott's Run.

0.5   **0.3**   Do *not* cross stream. (You may want to try the other side another day.) Bear right uphill and continue along stream.

0.6   **0.4**   Several trails intersect in small marshy area (small wooden bridge). *For a very scenic trail, but rocky and rough in spots:* Continue straight to stream edge and turn right on path there. Pass falls and continue to shore of Potomac. *For a more direct and easier route:* At junction of many trails, turn right on wide trail, then left at fork and left again to point where Scott's Run joins Potomac.

1.3   **0.8**   Potomac River; after enjoying view, retrace steps a few yards to wide trail leading uphill to left. (For route along river, see below.)

1.5   **0.9**   Fork in trail; bear left.

1.6   **1.0**   Chimney on left, just off main trail. This is the remains of the old homestead. On the trail to the right, opposite chimney and downhill, is the old swimming pool.

1.8   **1.1**   Take narrow trail leading left and downhill from saddle, before main trail begins to ascend. If you see trail leading to right, go back a few yards. This trail could be hard to locate, particularly in summer, but is easy to follow once found. At the fork go right and follow contours on bluffs above Potomac. (If you don't make this turn, continue straight on Burling Drive nearly a mile to a wide trail forking back to left. Follow this to overlook and continue directions below.)

2.4   **1.5**   Overlook; return to main trail, turn left, soon passing another overlook, then a stream.

2.9   **1.8**   Trail junction; turn right, climbing away from river.

3.2 **2.0** Cross trail; go straight.
3.4 **2.1** Turn left; wide trail forks to right.
3.7 **2.3** Trail junction; go right. Left leads to Va 193.
3.9 **2.4** Turn right, cross stream bed and turn right, or follow main trail as it circles head of stream and back to crossing.
4.0 **2.5** Trail junction; go left.
4.2 **2.6** Cross Burling Drive which leads right to homestead and left to Va 193.
4.7 **2.9** Pass several trails on right, then reach main junction; go left.
4.8 **3.0** At fork, go right.
5.2 **3.2** Parking lot.

Alternate route along river: From point where Scott's Run joins Potomac, stay on path along edge of river. In about 0.7 mi. (1.1 km.) path crosses rocks at base of outcrop on right. On other side of rocks, climb steeply uphill to right. At top, meet trail which goes a few feet right to overlook. Continue directions from 1.5 mi.

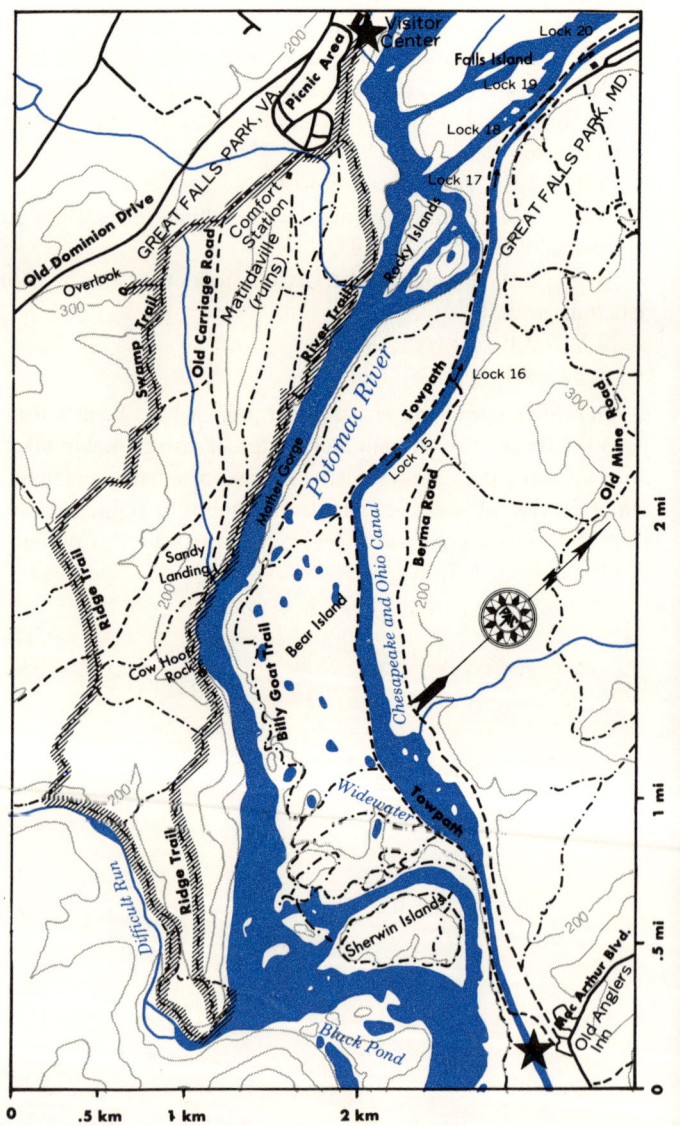

Hike No. 4
4 Difficult Run
Great Falls, Virginia

Length: 5.0 mi. (8.0 km.)
Elevation Change: Minimal.
PATC Map D.
Sketch map available at Visitor Center.
USGS Quads: Falls Church, Vienna, Va.

Variety is the word to describe this hike. Begin in Great Falls Park, with overlooks of the falls, and within a few minutes reach the Swamp Trail (prepare for insects in summer) where wild flowers and wildlife abound. Cross the ridge and descend steeply to Difficult Run. Here the trail may be rough and steep in spots, sometimes requiring a little rock scrambling as it winds to the Potomac River. Enjoy the cool water in summer or view the unusual ice formations in winter. After a steep climb to the ridge once again, the trail follows the rim of Mather Gorge as it leads back toward Great Falls—a channel believed to be 180 million years old. Nearly at the end of the circuit are the remains of the town of Matildaville, named by Lighthorse Harry Lee in honor of his wife, and the Potowmack Canal, planned by George Washington and operated for 26 years before being bought out by the Chesapeake and Ohio Company and abandoned.

Aside from the trails described above, there are others in the area worth exploring, including one running north along the river to the River Bend Nature Center.

Travel Directions: I-495 to Va 193 (Exit 13); travel west 4 mi. (6.4 km.) to Old Dominion Drive with blinker light and sign for Great Falls Park. Turn right, drive through main gate (small parking fee charged), and park in lot near Visitor Center.

Total Travel Distance: 5.4 mi. (8.9 km.)

Trail Data

km. mi.

0.0   0.0   Visitor Center; follow main path leading downstream and passing through picnic area.

0.5   0.3   Comfort Station; turn right, with Comfort Station on left, bear right at fork onto Old Carriage Road with gate across it.

0.8   0.5   Swamp Trail; turn right. Large rock outcrops to right and uphill offer overview of area. (In wet or buggy weather, avoid the Swamp Trail by hiking straight ahead on Old Carriage Rd. In about 0.5 mi. (0.8 km.) turn right onto wide path, pass other end of Swamp Trail, and continue straight to Ridge Trail.)

1.6   1.0   End of Swamp Trail; turn right onto wider trail and climb to top of ridge.

2.1   1.3   Ridge trail; turn left at small fenced area on left and pass several narrow trails leading left and right.

2.4   1.5   Cross horse trail; go straight ahead and up embankment; at top bear right onto wide trail.

2.6   1.6   At top of rise, bear right onto narrow trail and soon begin steep descent to Difficult Run. Near beginning of descent enjoy view from overhanging cliff but *stay away from edge*.

3.1   1.9   Difficult Run; go left and follow wide path along stream. At the top of a rise, where wide path climbs above the stream, a narrow trail bears right to an alternate lower route.

3.9   2.4   Pass Ridge Trail leading to left. (Return to this trail to continue circuit after reaching Potomac.)

4.2   2.6   Difficult Run joins the Potomac River; sandy beach. After enjoying the view, retrace steps up hill to Ridge Trail.

4.5   2.8   Ridge Trail; turn right and climb to top of ridge. Bear left at top and follow wide trail, blue-blazed. Pass horse trail leading left to Difficult Run.

5.3 **3.3** Turn right onto narrow trail, still blue-blazed.

5.6 **3.5** Cow Hoof Rock; overlook of Potomac. Turn left at post and descend. Cow Hoof Rocks are to right.

6.0 **3.7** Cross stream and swing to left.

6.1 **3.8** Trail junction; turn right about 25 ft. then left. Hard surfaced road to right leads downhill to Sandy Landing.

6.6 **4.1** Bear left at gorge entrance to Potowmack Canal; iron hooks and holes for blasting still remain. Walk on either side of Canal past locks and come into broad flat area, formerly the "holding basin". The ruins of Matildaville are nearby.

7.1 **4.4** Cross stream on footbridge and continue on wide path.

7.6 **4.7** Picnic area; continue straight ahead.

8.0 **5.0** Visitor Center.

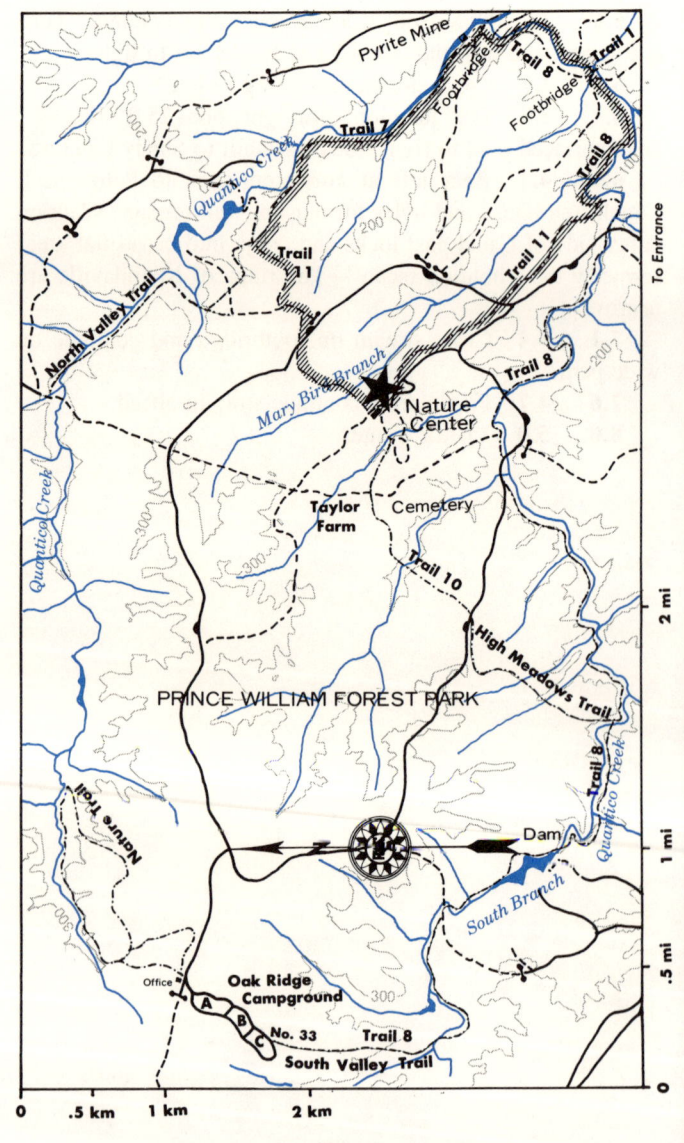

Hike No. 5

5 Pyrite Mine Loop
Prince William Forest Park, Virginia

Length: 6.0 mi. (9.7 km.)
Elevation Change: Minimal; level terrain interspersed with short, steep ascents and descents.
Sketch map available at Nature Center.
USGS Quad: Joplin, Va.

Prince William Park offers over 35 miles of hiking trails, much of this distance along the north and south branches of Quantico Creek. The terrain is pleasantly rolling and most of the walking is not difficult. Although there are no spectacular views from lofty mountain peaks, there is much more subtle beauty for those willing to look for it. Here is the place to watch the forest come alive with new growth in the early spring. Here is the place to watch its last blaze of glory before it goes to rest for the winter. Here is a place to find quiet and solitude, to stare up at majestic old oaks, poplars and pines, to look down upon moss, partridge berry and ferns, to pass through the laurel and the holly. Here is a place to study the work of the beavers, to study the stages of natural succession in the forest, to look for deer, to enjoy a ripe pawpaw if you can find one the squirrels have missed.

The hike begins at the Nature Center and winds through the woods before meeting and following the South Fork of Quantico Creek. Watch for signs of beaver activity along the streams. About midway the site of the old pyrite mine is crossed. Just beyond this site on the left and uphill you may find the concrete foundations of the locomotive sheds, machine shop, engine room, boiler room, tracks and trestles dating back to the late 1800's and early 1900's when iron ore was hauled from here by train. Further along a large outcropping of rocks in the stream offers a good spot for lunch or a rest. These trails are all well-worn with much of the walking on nearly level terrain broken by an occasional short, steep ascent and descent.

Travel Directions: I-495 to I-95; south on I-95 to Triangle-Quantico Exit, also sign for Prince William Forest Park; turn right onto Va 619 and in a few hundred feet turn right onto entrance road for park. Follow signs to Nature Center.

Total Travel Distance: 24 mi. (39 km.)

Trail Data

km. *mi.*

0.0 **0.0** Nature Center; follow road leading straight from front of Nature Center.

0.2 **0.1** Turn left from road onto Trail 11, marked by concrete post and dark blue blazes.

1.3 **0.8** Cross hardtop road and continue on Trail 11.

2.6 **1.6** Junction with Trail 8, white-blazed; go left along South Quantico Creek. At next junction, as trail branches left and right along stream, turn to left.

3.9 **2.4** Junction with wide trail; turn right, still on T-8.

4.0 **2.5** Suspension bridge on right; cross bridge and turn left along stream, still T-8.

5.0 **3.1** Suspension bridge, on left; recross stream and turn right, still T-8 and white-blazed.

5.2 **3.2** Dirt road; turn left about 100 ft. then right and downhill on Trail 7, blue-blazed and marked by post. Pass site of pyrite mine and locomotive shed.

7.2 **4.5** Rock outcropping in stream.

7.4 **4.6** Cross small bridge and turn left uphill away from stream.

7.7 **4.8** Meet Trail 11 again and go left, dark blue blazes.

8.4 **5.2** Turn left on old dirt road.

8.5 **5.3** Leave road and go right at post, still Trail 11.

8.7 **5.4** Cross Park Central Drive, paved.

9.5 **5.9** Dirt road; turn left.

9.7 **6.0** Nature Center.

Hike No. 6
6 Beaver Loop
Prince William Forest Park, Virginia

Length: 7.5 mi. (12.1 km.)
Elevation Change: Minimal.
Map available at Nature Center.
USGS Quads: Joplin, Quantico, Va.

In the 1600's the land now covered by the park was a prosperous farming and lumbering community, supplying the busy port of Dumfries. In time, the lack of good conservation practices led to heavy erosion and poor soil, eventually causing the area to be abandoned. The forest you'll be walking through now is in various stages of recovery from those years of abuse. The trees are mostly oak, hickory and beech with isolated stands of pine and an understory of holly, laurel, dogwood and redbud.

Geographically, Prince William Park literally straddles the "fall line", the point where the rolling hills of the Piedmont Plateau drop off to the flat Coastal Plain. The first and last sections of this hike are through the deciduous woods of the rolling Piedmont terrain, while the central section follows the bank of South Branch Quantico Creek as it tumbles over the rocks cutting its way to the Potomac. A watchful eye will detect the presence of beavers in numerous spots along the stream. Although you're not likely to see one of the furry fellows, the indiscriminately felled trees and the pointed stumps are sure signs that they're nearby, or have been in the past.

A sidetrip can be made by walking approximately one mile upstream to the dam and the lake.

Travel Directions: I-495 to I-95; south on I-95 to Triangle-Quantico Exit, also sign for Prince William Forest Park; turn right onto Va 619 and in a few hundred feet turn right onto entrance road for park. Follow signs to Nature Center.
Total Travel Distance: 24 mi. (39 km.)

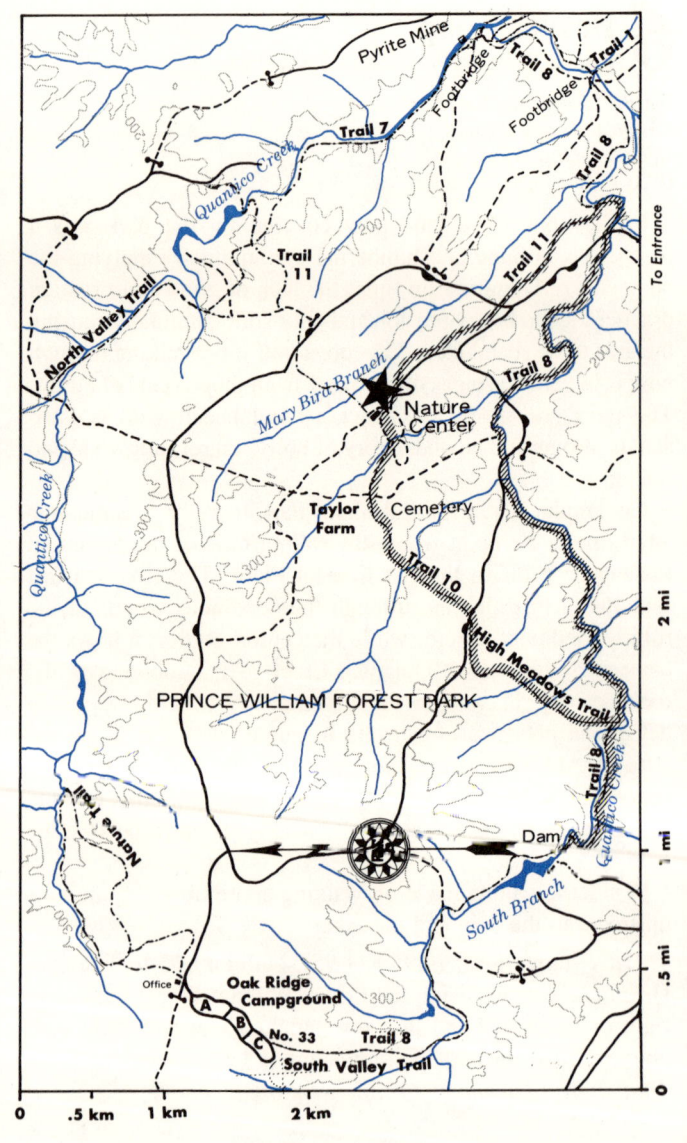

Trail Data

km.   *mi.*

0.0   **0.0**   Nature Center; facing building, walk along "Old Black Top Road" to right, passing water tower.

0.2   **0.1**   Turn left onto T-10, orange-blazed and marked with concrete post.

0.3   **0.2**   Cross footbridge and turn right immediately.

0.6   **0.4**   Cross T-7, formerly main road through area when it was a farm community. Enter cleared area, site of Taylor family farm and local store; pass small cemetery on left.

2.3   **1.4**   Cross Scenic Drive.

3.5   **2.2**   Reach South Branch Quantico Creek. (If you want to make the sidetrip to the lake, cross the bridge here and follow the white-blazed trail upstream about a mile.) To continue circuit, do *not* cross bridge. Continue straight ahead on white-blazed T-8, and follow creek for next 3.5 miles (5.6 km.). Look for beaver activity all along this section.

6.4   **4.0**   Cross Scenic Drive.

6.6   **4.1**   T-7 forks to left; bear right and continue on T-8.

7.1   **4.4**   Walk under Scenic Drive on footbridge.

9.0   **5.6**   Cross Park Central Road.

9.5   **5.9**   Turn left onto T-11, blazed dark blue.

10.8   **6.7**   Cross Scenic Drive.

11.9   **7.4**   Turn right on road to Nature Center.

12.1   **7.5**   Nature Center.

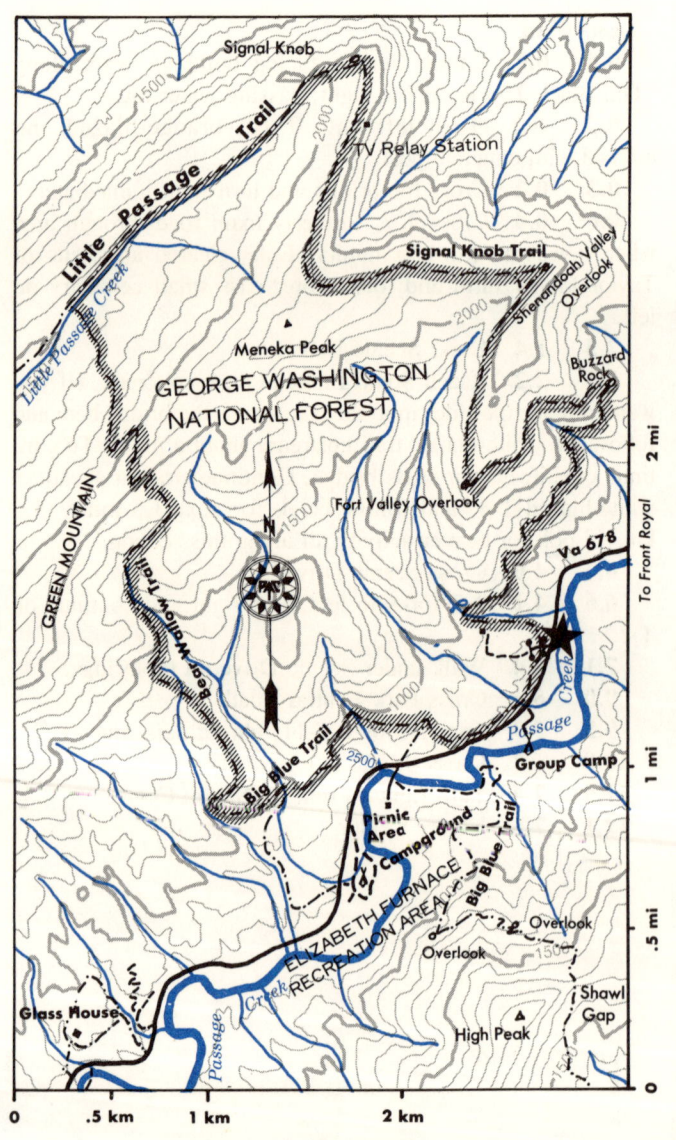

Hike No. 7

7 Signal Knob
Massanutten Mountain, Virginia

Length: 10.6 mi. (17.1 km.)
Elevation Change: Approx. 1600 ft.
PATC Map G.
USGS Quad: Strasburg, Va.

The Signal Knob circuit originates in Elizabeth Furnace Recreation Area, the site of a charcoal-blast iron furnace built in 1836. During the Civil War it supplied pigiron to Tredegar Iron Works in Richmond, noted for some of the finest cannons used by the Confederacy. At the top of the ridge is Signal Knob, used as a Confederate lookout to monitor the movements of Federal troops in the Shenandoah Valley. The signal was relayed along the ridge until it eventually reached Richmond.

From Signal Knob the trail winds along the ridge then gradually descends, passing two more viewpoints before returning to the starting point. All trails are graded and easy to follow, although some are quite rocky.

Travel Directions: I-495 to I-66; I-66 west to Front Royal exit via US 340; US 340 south to Va 55; Va 55 west to SR 678; SR 678 south (left) 3.5 mi. (5.6 km.) to small parking area on right, by sign for Signal Knob Trail and Bear Wallow Trail.

Total Travel Distance: 70 mi. (113 km.)

Trail Data

km. *mi.*

0.0   0.0   At rear of parking area pass gate and immediately turn left onto Bear Wallow Trail with white blazes. (Turn left just after large boulder.)

0.3   0.2   Approach hard-surfaced road on left; walk parallel to road for short distance then bear right uphill, with white blazes.

0.8   0.5   Junction with blue-blazed Big Blue Trail

coming in from left; continue straight on trail with both blue and white blazes.

2.1 **1.3** Cross stream and follow blue-blazed trail straight ahead. White blazes lead left to road.

6.4 **4.0** Top of Green Mountain Ridge; descend to Little Passage Creek.

7.7 **4.8** Cross Little Passage Creek and turn right onto wide trail with orange blazes; blue-blazed trail leads left 1 mi. (1.6 km.) to Strasburg Reservoir.

9.5 **5.9** Near top of ridge, stay left on orange-blazed trail to Signal Knob Overlook.

9.7 **6.0** Signal Knob overlooking Strasburg; follow along ridge to right, now using yellow-blazed Signal Knob Trail.

10.0 **6.2** Pass UHF Channel 70 relay station on left.

12.2 **7.6** Trail goes left to Shenandoah Valley Overlook, now very much overgrown.

13.5 **8.4** Fort Valley Overlook.

14.5 **9.0** Buzzard Rock Overlook.

16.4 **10.2** Covered spring on right of trail where trail makes sharp switchback to left.

17.1 **10.6** Signal Knob Parking Area.

Hike No. 8
8 Duncan Knob
Massanutten Mountain, Virginia

Length: 7.3 mi. (11.8 km.)
Elevation Change: Approx. 2000 ft.
PATC Map G.
USGS Quad: Hamburg, Va.

The high point, literally and figuratively, of this hike is Duncan Knob, a rocky peak with an uninterrupted view, located along the ridge of Catback Mountain. The circuit begins in Crisman Hollow and climbs to Peach Orchard Gap. Before the trail begins to descend, a short easy bushwhack to the left (north) will lead to Duncan Knob with exceptional views from its rocky ledges. From here the trail descends into Duncan Hollow where it follows the stream south, then turns to cross Middle Mountain. At the top of the ridge another bushwhack (this one's about a mile) will end at Strickler Knob with its microwave reflector and another good view. Several wildlife clearings and ponds are passed, with much evidence of deer, before the trail closes the loop of the circuit and returns to the parking area.

Travel Directions: I-495 to I-66; I-66 west to Gainesville then west on US 29 to Warrenton; right on US 211; cross Skyline Drive and continue on US 211 to New Market Gap. Pass Massanutten Visitor Center on left and just beyond turn right onto gravel road, FDR 274. (Check speedometer to help in locating trailhead.) At 0.3 mi. (0.5 km.) pass Massanutten Story Trail with nice view at end. Continue past sign on right for Scothorn Gap Trail. In 6.3 mi. (10.1 km.) reach Peach Orchard Gap Trail on right. The sign may be gone but the post remains. The trail is wide, goes off at an angle, and has a parking pull-off at the head of it. It is blue-blazed.

Note: FDR 274 may be closed for a week or two in early spring to avoid damage to road during spring breakup, usually late Feb. and early March.

Total Travel Distance: 97 mi. (156 km.)

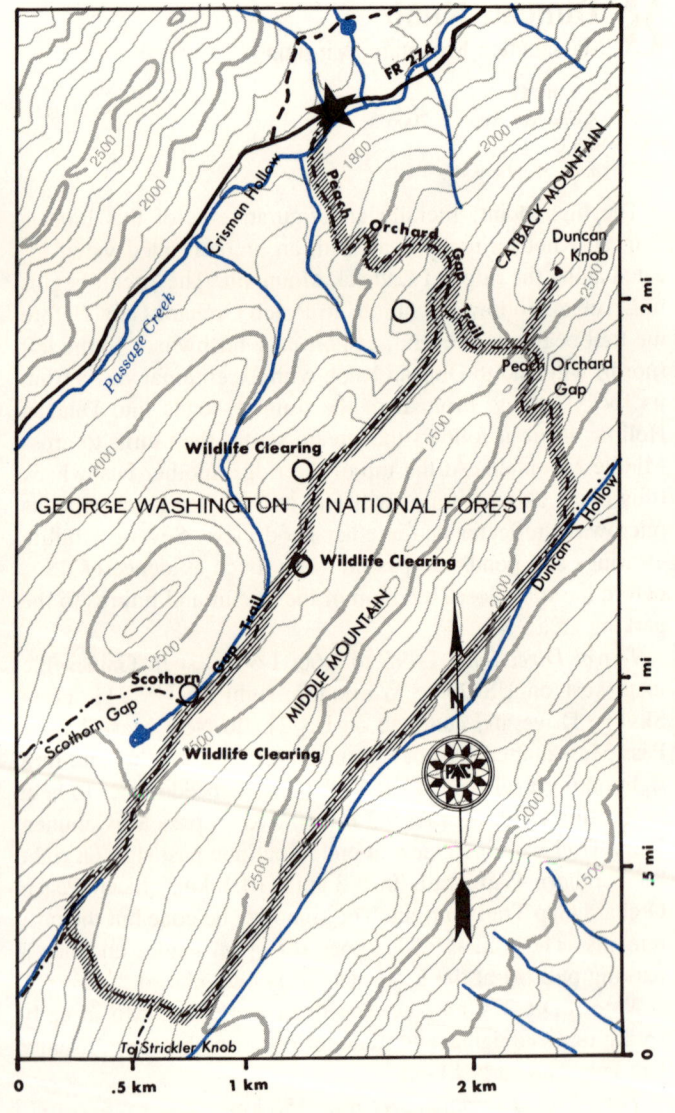

Trail Data

km. mi.

0.0 0.0 Peach Orchard Gap Trail, blue-blazed; turn south (right from road).

0.2 0.1 Cross stream and bear left on trail with switchback.

1.6 1.0 Junction with red-blazed trail; continue straight on blue-blazed trail.

2.1 1.3 High point in Peach Orchard Gap; bushwhack left (north) to Duncan Knob for excellent view. Follow ridge through woods for short distance until rocks come into sight. Watch carefully how you approach the rocky knob so you can return the same say. Better still, use a compass. Finding the way back can be tricky. Return to Peach Orchard Gap Trail and turn left.

3.2 2.0 Reach Duncan Hollow. Turn right onto orange-blazed Massanutten Mountain East Trail and ascend gradually.

6.1 3.8 Crest of ridge. A rather long and rough bushwhack to left along ridge will bring you to more overlooks and eventually Strickler Knob at end of ridge.

6.8 4.2 Junction with yellow-blazed trail; turn right.

7.9 4.9 Merge with red-blazed Scothorn Gap Trail entering from left at wildlife clearing; keep right.

8.5 5.3 Pond on right.

8.9 5.5 Wildlife clearing; skirt to right.

10.0 6.2 Wildlife clearing on left.

10.1 6.3 Junction with blue-blazed Peach Orchard Gap Trail; turn left.

11.6 7.2 Cross stream.

11.8 7.3 Parking area.

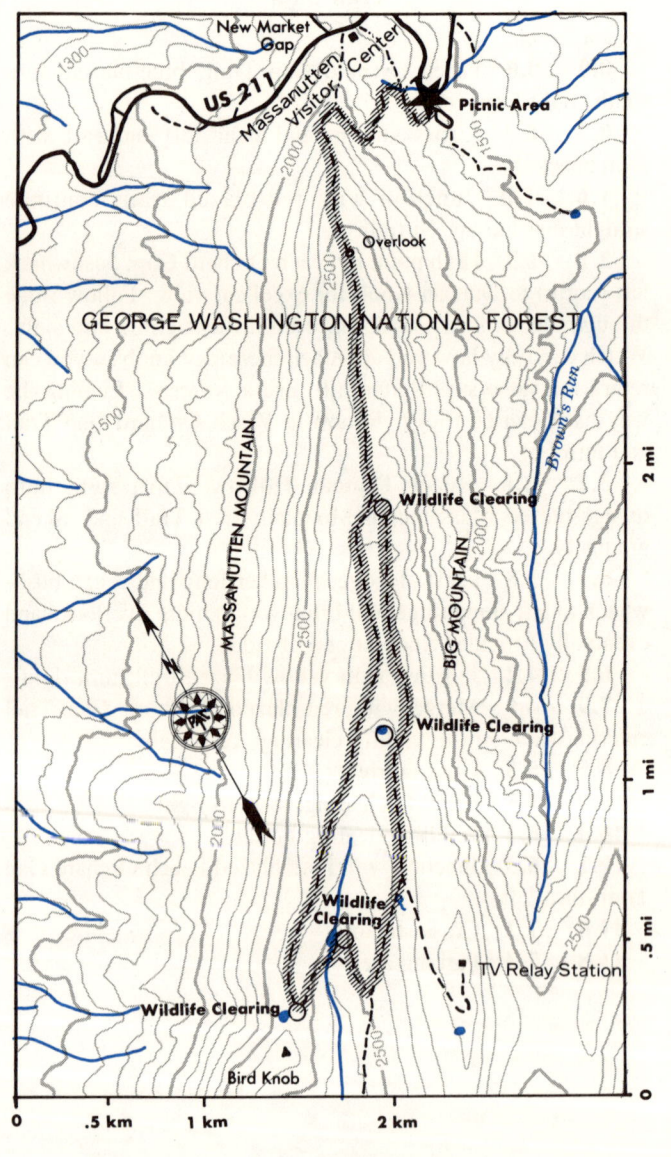

Hike No. 9
9 Bird Knob
Massanutten Mountain, Virginia

Length: 8.5 mi. (13.7 km.)
Elevation Change: Approx. 1000 ft.
PATC Map H.
USGS Quads: Tenth Legion, Stanley, Hamburg, Va.

After climbing steadily out of New Market Gap, the Bird Knob Trail reaches the rocky crest of the Massanutten. The horizontal rock formations are rather unusual and the view from the ledges includes the ridges in West Virginia. The trail passes through teaberry and laurel along the nearly level ridge before reaching the wildlife clearing at the base of Bird Knob. A pond in the far corner is abundant with wildlife, especially in early spring. From here the trail crosses to another ridge, skirts a crystal clear pond and passes below the summit bearing the relay station for TV Channel 75. Still with little change in elevation the trail rejoins the original ridge just before the rock ledges with a second opportunity for views at a different time of day, then descends steeply to New Market Gap.

Travel Directions: I-495 to I-66; I-66 west to Gainesville; US 29 west to Warrenton, then west (right) on US 211 crossing Skyline Drive at Panaroma. Turn left into New Market Gap Forest Service Picnic Ground just before reaching Visitor Center. In 0.1 mi. (0.2 km.), where road splits, pass sign for trail on right. Park just beyond.

Total Travel Distance: 77 mi. (124 km.)

Trail Data

km.   mi.

0.0   0.0   Orange-blazed trail leaves west side of road, at point where road splits.

0.3   0.2   Turn left and follow orange blazes. Straight ahead (white-blazed) leads to Visitor Center. (Hike may be started from there.)

1.0 **0.6** Trail entering right; red-blazed boundary markers; keep left.

1.3 **0.8** Large boulders on left; trail swings left then climbs steeply to ridge.

2.1 **1.3** Series of rocky ledges with excellent views to west.

3.5 **2.2** Where orange blazes turn left to wildlife clearing, continue straight ahead on narrow trail; pick up white blazes, following west ridge to wildlife clearing.

6.3 **3.9** Wildlife clearing. (Bird Knob is straight ahead across clearing. The three knobs can be easily bushwhacked but offer very limited views. The pond in the corner may be of more interest.) Bear left along edge of clearing to dirt road leading off NE corner, still white-blazed.

6.9 **4.3** Road to left leads few hundred feet to wildlife clearing and crystal clear pond.

7.1 **4.4** Meet gravel road leading to TV station; turn left, and follow orange blazes for remainder of hike.

7.9 **4.9** Bear left onto overgrown woods road, leaving gravel road which continues right 0.6 mi. (1.0 km.) to relay station. Look for giant anthills along this stretch.

8.4 **5.2** Road splits; skirt left edge of clearing and follow orange blazes.

9.8 **6.1** Wildlife clearing; skirt left edge of clearing and follow orange blazes. At trail junction turn right. This completes the loop.

11.3 **7.0** Rock ledges; begin descent.

12.7 **7.9** Red property boundary blazes; keep right.

13.4 **8.3** Trail splits; keep right. (Left goes to Visitor Center.)

13.7 **8.5** Picnic area.

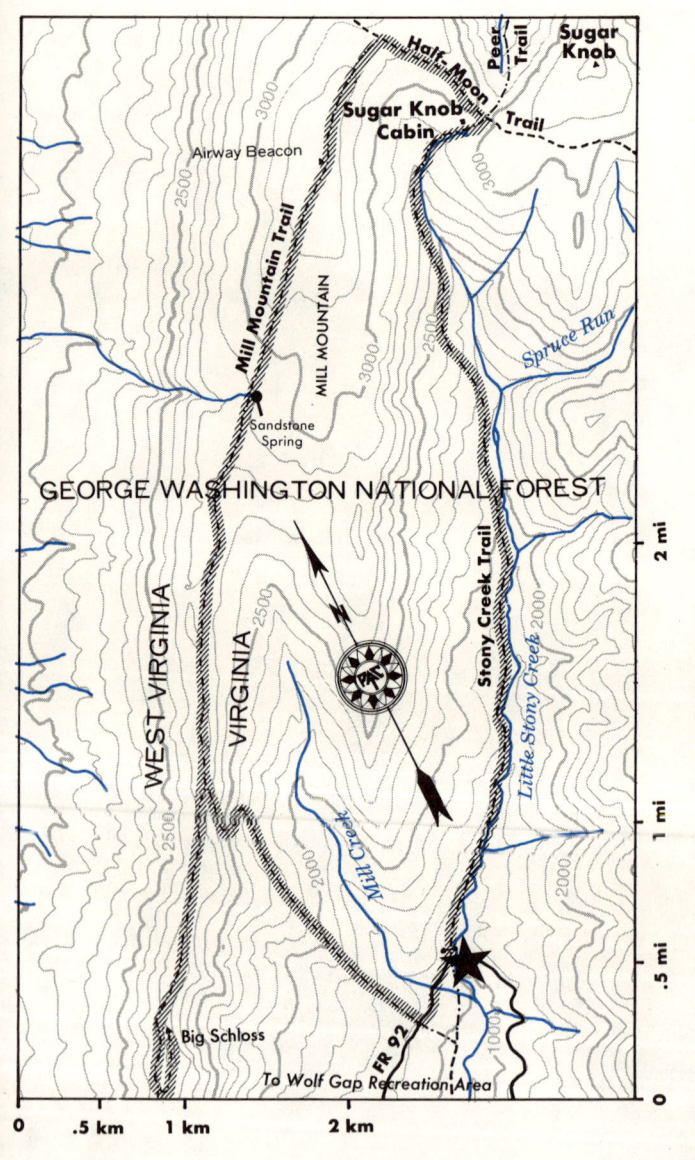

10 Hike No. 10
Big Schloss
Great North Mountain, Virginia—West Virginia

Length: 12.0 mi. (19.3 km.)
Elevation Change: Approx. 1800 ft.
PATC Map F.
USGS Quads: Wolf Gap, Woodstock, Va.-WVa.

Undoubtedly one of the loveliest areas around! This hike will take you through the varied conditions of an everchanging forest. From a beginning along a clear, bubbling trout stream lined with giant hemlocks and a path of moss and rocks, you'll climb onto the ridge with its dense low growth of laurel and scrub oak, walking on a sandy footpath with giant anthills along the sides. You'll find mature deciduous woods with a grassy carpet and later a dense undergrowth. Pass many rocky ledges culminating in the largest outcropping known as Big Schloss, named by early German settlers and meaning "castle" in their language. Here you may eat your lunch in two states at the same time, since the Virginia-West Virginia line bisects the top of the ridge—and the panoramic view is beyond description.

In May the woods are full of iris, azaleas and orchids which give way to the laurel in June. Then there's the cool shade and breeze in summer—and don't miss the brilliant colors of fall—or the snow covered trails of winter with the interesting little animal tracks scurrying here and there. In other words, it's a hike for all seasons.

The trail is nearly level at first, then narrows and climbs steadily to Sugar Knob Cabin (a PATC cabin). From here it ascends more gradually then follows the ridge of Mill Mountain, climbing finally to Big Schloss. The trail descending the ridge is steep at points and narrow, as it "zigzags" (longer than switchbacks) down to the forest road.

Travel Directions: I-495 to I-66; I-66 west to I-81; south on I-81 to Va 42 marked Woodstock; south on Va 42 to Columbia

Furnace (do not go towards Woodstock); right (west) onto SR 675 in Columbia Furnace. Cross creek and bear left. At fork, bear right, still on SR 675. At FDR 92 turn right about 4 miles (6.4 km.) to parking lot on right, just before crossing Little Stony Creek.

Note: FDR 92 may be closed for a week or two in early spring to avoid damage to road during spring breakup, usually late Feb. and early March.

Total Travel Distance: 103 mi. (165 km.)

Trail Data

km.   *mi.*

0.0   **0.0**   Follow yellow-blazed Stony Creek Trail uphill toward Sugar Knob Cabin (marked by sign). Watch for switchbacks near top.

5.8   **3.6**   Spring on right.

6.0   **3.7**   Sugar Knob Cabin. This is a cabin owned by PATC and available for use by reservation only.

6.1   **3.8**   Half-Moon Trail (also part of Big Blue Trail) with blue blazes; go left. Watch for giant anthills here.

6.9   **4.3**   Mill Mountain Trail, orange-blazed; go left.

7.9   **4.9**   Old FAA beacon on right, now a solar powered Forest Service radio repeater.

9.3   **5.8**   Sandstone Spring; dependable. A little further along the ridge watch for rocky outcroppings which offer excellent views, particularly if you choose the shortened route, omitting Big Schloss.

12.4   **7.7**   Blue-blazed trail forks left downhill by rock cairn; continue straight ahead for Big Schloss. For a shorter hike, turn left here, descend 1.3 mi. (2.1 km.) to FDR 92 and turn left to car. (0.4 mi. (0.6 km.)

13.2   **8.2**   Base of Big Schloss; continue straight ahead passing below rocks.

13.8   **8.6**   Trail to Big Schloss, white-blazed, doubles back to left.

14.3 **8.9** Overlook! Be sure to go all the way to the end.

14.8 **9.2** Return to orange-blazed Mill Mountain Trail and turn right. Be careful here as it is easy to merge with trail before realizing you're on it.

16.1 **10.0** Turn sharp right onto Big Schloss Cut-Off Trail which is blue-blazed and marked by a rock cairn. Trail descends via two major switchbacks, then becomes less steep.

18.0 **11.2** Several large anthills and charcoal hearths beside trail between here and road.

18.7 **11.6** FDR 92; turn left

19.3 **12.0** Parking area.

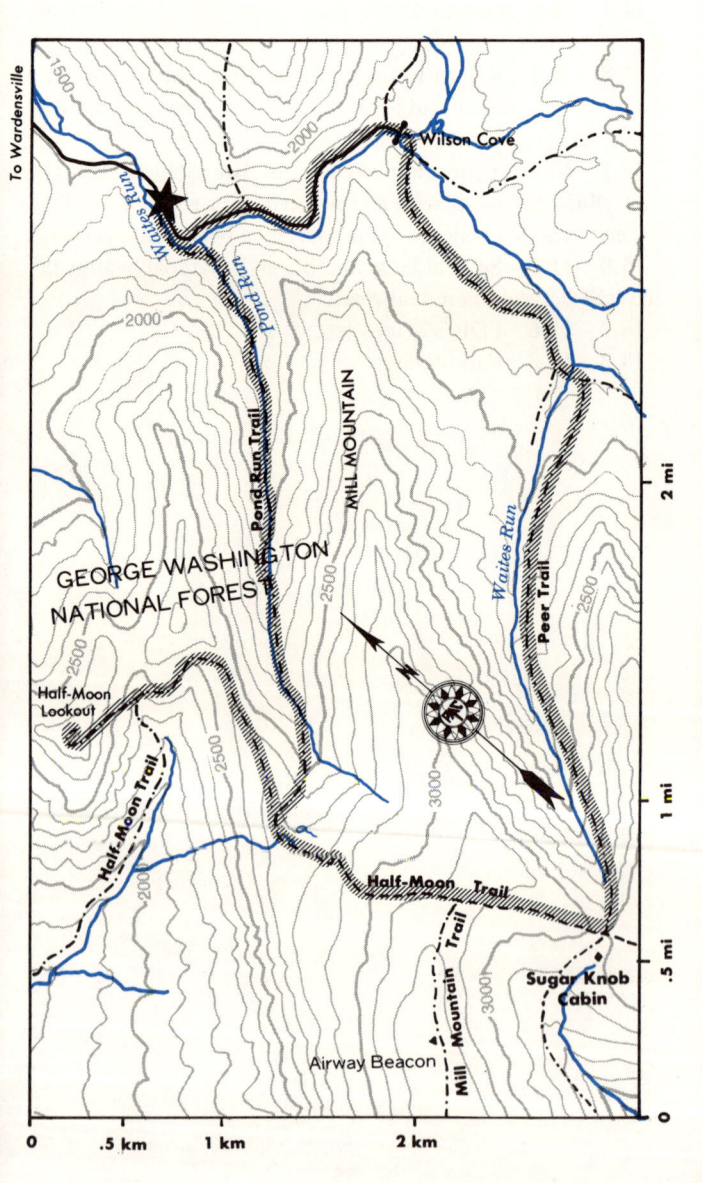

Hike No. 11

11 Pond Run-Half-Moon Lookout
Great North Mountain, Virginia—West Virginia

Length: 10.8 mi. (17.4 km.)
Elevation Change: Approx. 1600 ft.
PATC Map F.
USGS Quads: Baker, W.Va., Wolf Gap, Wardensville, Woodstock, Va.-W.Va.

From its beginning along Waites Run the trail climbs, steeply at times, on a rough footway, through the gorge of Pond Run, crossing the stream a total of eight times. Once on the ridge a side trip to Half-Moon Lookout, site of an old firetower, gives a spectacular view down the valley between Mill Mountain and Long Mountain. Returning along the ridge the trail passes a spring, climbs a bit more as it nears Sugar Knob, then descends via the Peer Trail along the eastern side of Waites Run. The final stretch skirts high pastures, then follows a road through private property logged in 1982-1983. The owners don't object to hikers so long as they don't litter, camp or build fires; however, the cows in the lower pastures may make you feel otherwise! Return through Wilson's Cove.

Travel Directions: I-495 to I-66; I-66 to I-81; I-81 south to Strasburg exit, marked US 11 to Va 55; follow US 11 to Va 55 which turns right in Strasburg; Va 55 west. Cross West Virginia line and continue on Va 55 until just *before* junction with W.Va. 259 east of Wardensville. Turn left at Jct. 259 *sign* (not at 259). Go to end of road, turn left and immediately right. (This road passes a Community Park on the left and eventually turns into a rather rough dirt road.) In 5.6 mi. (9.0 km.) reach Pond Run Trail on right (blue-blazed).

Total Travel Distance: 95 mi. (153 km.)

Trail Data

km. *mi.*

0.0 **0.0** Follow blue-blazed Pond Run Trail to right (south). This is also part of the Big Blue Trail. If crossing

Waites Run looks tricky, walk back downstream on Waites Run Rd. and cross on road bridge. Walk back along stream to blue-blazed trail which soon turns to the right and climbs steeply along Pond Run.

3.7 **2.3** Junction with yellow-blazed Half-Moon Trail; signs; turn right.

4.7 **2.9** Leave Half-Moon trail and bear right onto white-blazed trail to Half-Moon Lookout.

6.0 **3.7** Half-Moon Lookout site with remains of old fire tower. Retrace steps to intersection with Half-Moon Trail.

7.2 **4.5** Merge with yellow-blazed Half-Moon Trail.

8.2 **5.1** Junction with Pond Run Trail. Continue straight ahead with blue blazes.

8.5 **5.3** Cross stream and come to enclosed spring on left, just before ascending.

10.0 **6.0** Pass Mill Mountain Trail on right.

10.5 **6.5** Intersection with purple-blazed Peer Trail; go left. (Sugar Knob Cabin and spring are on yellow trail to right approx. 100 yds and 250 yds). Descend steeply at first, then more gradually.

13.5 **8.4** Enter private property; follow logging road. Don't litter and keep dogs leashed - cows ahead. Follow blazes through pasture and past farm buildings.

15.8 **9.8** Pass through iron gates to Waites Run Road; turn left.

17.4 **10.8** Parking area.

Hike No. 12

12 Little Sluice Mtn.-White Rock Cliff

Great North Mountain, Virginia—West Virginia

Length: 11.6 mi. (18.7 km.) or 13.8 mi. (22.2 km.)
Elevation Change: Approx. 1400 ft.
PATC Map F.
USGS Quads: Wolf Gap, Woodstock, Va.-W.Va.

This hike offers several options, with the possibility of two dayhikes, one long dayhike, or an overnight. It begins on an old lumber road along Narrow Passage Creek then crosses over into the watershed of Cedar Creek. From here it joins the Big Blue Trail and climbs 1400 feet up the northeast slope of Little Sluice Mountain. Once this climb is over and the ridge attained, the rest of the trip is gentle woodland trail with slight ups and downs, and one steady descent at the end. About midway, a white-blazed trail leads 0.3 mi. (0.5 km.) to the open rocky ledges known as White Rock Cliff. Further on there is another viewpoint on the right and a reliable piped spring near the remains of an old cabin. The final portion of the hike follows the old "Bread Road", reportedly used to haul "bread" (food and supplies) to workers at the charcoal hearths.

For those with the time and energy to explore a little, an additional 2.2 mi. (3.5 km.) roundtrip, will take you to Little Sluice. The walking is easy except for the final scramble to the top of the rocks. A second circuit can be made by ascending the Bread Road Trail and either returning the same way or via Little Sluice Road, a steeper and rougher descent.

Travel Directions: I-495 to I-66; I-66 west to I-81; south on I-81 to Va 42 marked Woodstock; south on Va 42 to Columbia Furnace (do not go towards Woodstock); right (west) onto SR 675 in Columbia Furnace. In about 1 mile (1.6 km.) turn right onto SR 608 which soon becomes FDR 88. Continue to gate blocking road and park. If road is rough here, return 0.1 mi.

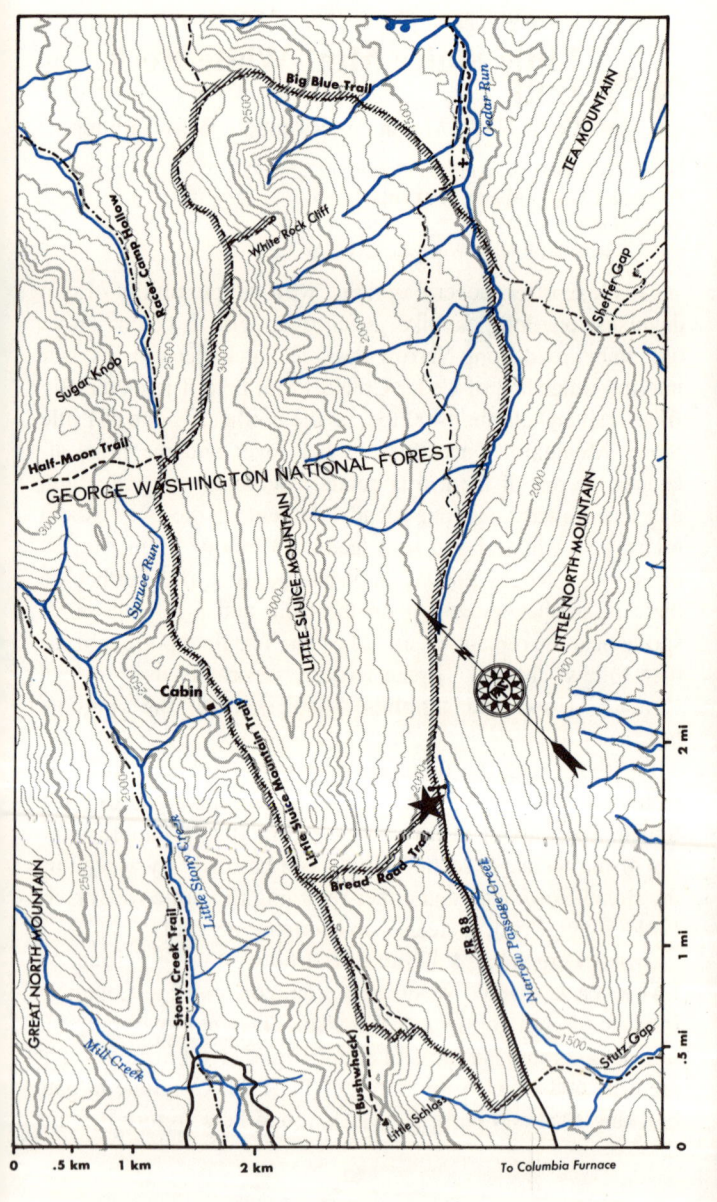

(0.2 km.) to pulloff at foot of red-blazed trail.

Note: FDR 88 may be closed for a week or two in early spring to avoid damage to road during spring breakup, usually late Feb. and early March.

Total Travel Distance: 99 mi. (159 km.)

Trail Data

km. mi.

0.0 0.0 Pass gate at end of FDR 88 and continue straight ahead, through logged area, following yellow blazes.

2.5 1.6 Trail intersects Cedar Creek Road in a clear cut. Continue on road with yellow blazes.

5.3 3.3 Left on Big Blue Trail with blue blazes.

6.6 4.1 Cross stream and continue straight; old road goes to right.

8.5 5.3 Intersect and follow old Sulphur Spring Gap Road to left, still following blue blazes.

9.3 5.8 Sulphur Spring Gap; W.Va.-Va. state line follows top of main ridge. Bear left on blue-blazed trail. Old road to right descends to Wilson's Cove. This is the old Mail Path used many years ago as the mail route from Woodstock, Va to Wardensville, W.Va.

10.1 6.3 White Rock Cliff Trail on left, marked by white blazes; cliffs are 0.3 mi. (0.5 km.) downhill.

11.1 6.9 Overlook on right; Racer Camp Hollow and Sugar Knob.

12.2 7.6 Leave Big Blue Trail and turn to left onto purple-blazed Little Sluice Trail (jeep road).

12.9 8.0 Cross Spruce Run.

14.5 9.0 Remains of hunter's cabin on right.

14.7 9.1 Reliable spring on left. Continue along road, still purple blazed. Curve to left. (Vandals in this area amuse themselves by removing blazes so they may be sparse.)

16.6 10.3 Wildlife clearing to right of trail.

16.7 10.4 In broad, flat area, just beyond wildlife clearing on right, turn left onto orange-blazed Bread Road Trail.

Caution: Orange blazes may not be visible at junction. This junction is also marked by a pile of rocks on left of Little Sluice Trail. (For side trip to Little Sluice, see below.)

18.5   **11.5**   Reach FDR 88 and turn left.

18.7   **11.6**   Gate and parking area.

Optional Side Trip to Little Sluice

For a spectacular view of the surrounding area, hike an additional 2.2 mi. (3.5 km.) roundtrip to Little Sluice (or Schloss, German for castle) so named because of its resemblance to a stone castle on the mountain. Instead of turning left at the Bread Road Trail, continue straight ahead 0.7 mi. (1.1 km.) to a wildlife clearing where the main road bends left. Cross the clearing, passing huge spruce trees and turn right (southwest) onto ridge, still on old road which becomes footpath, then more or less disappears. Follow ridge, easy walking, about 0.3 mi. (0.5 km.) until a huge rock heap appears before you. This is Little Schloss, a formation similar to Big Schloss on the ridge to the west. If you enjoy a little rock scrambling, the higher you get, the better the view. Return to the Bread Road Trail, turn right downhill, as described above.

Bread Road-Little Sluice Circuit

If time or energy prevent you from making the trip to Little Sluice on the previous hike, come back another day for this circuit. Park as described in original hike.

km.   *mi.*

0.0   **0.0**   From FDR 88, ascend orange-blazed Bread Road Trail.

1.8   **1.1**   Reach Little Sluice Trail, a wide jeep road, purple-blazed in spots. Turn left.

2.9   **1.8**   Continue straight ahead through wildlife clearing as main road veers left downhill. See above for description of route to rocks.

3.5   **2.2**   Little Sluice. Scramble to the top, but do it carefully. Return to wildlife clearing by same route.

4.2   **2.6**   Wildlife clearing. Pass spruce trees and continue to main jeep road. Follow this road downhill to right. Pass logged area near bottom.

6.3   **3.9**   FDR 88. Turn left and follow road.

9.2   **5.7**   Parking area.

This circuit involves a rather steep descent on a rocky forest service road, and a 1.8 (mi. (2.9 km.) walk along the nearly level FDR 88. A shorter, less steep hike could be made by both ascending and descending on the Bread Road Trail. (4.4 mi.-7.1 km.)

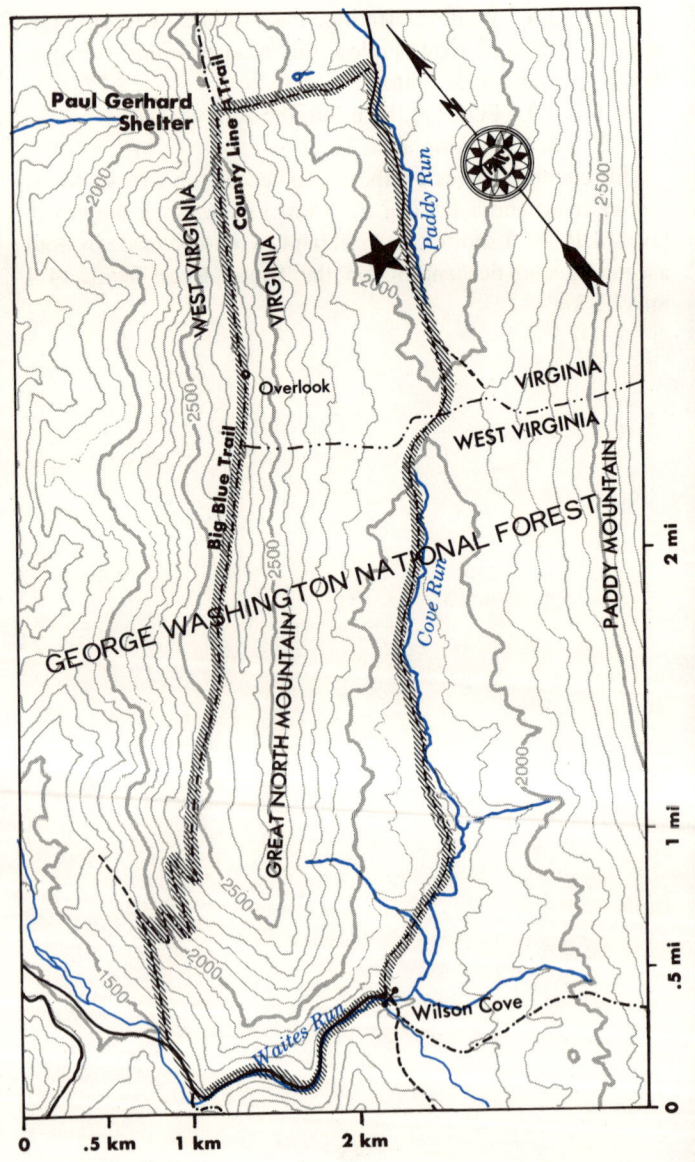

Hike No. 13
13 Big Blue-Cove Run
Great North Mountain, Virginia—West Virginia

Length: 9.0 mi. (14.5 km.)
Elevation Change: Approx. 1400 ft.
PATC Map F.
USGS Quad: Wardensville, Va.-W.Va.

The first section of this hike follows an old lumber road paralleling Paddy Run which flows north, then ascends slightly to the headwaters of Cove Run and follows it as it flows south. In Wilson's Cove, a small farm area, the route turns west for a short distance along a dirt road before striking out to the north on the County Line Trail, part of the Big Blue Trail, which follows the Virginia-West Virginia state line. After climbing steadily by switchbacks, the trail levels, then climbs more gradually, reaching the crest of the ridge just before the Paul Gerhard Shelter. There are many opportunities for views along here from the rocky ridge just to the east (right) of the trail. At the shelter another blue-blazed trail leads steeply downhill to the forest road and thus back to the car. The woods in this section are filled with laurel, azaleas, blueberries, etc. In fall the colors are some of the most brilliant in the area. Water may sometimes be found to the left of the trail in the col below the shelter, after the steep descent.

Travel Directions: I-495 to I-81; I-81 south to exit marked Strasburg-US 11 to Va 55. Follow US 11 to Va 55 in Strasburg; turn right (west) onto Va 55 and go about 14 miles; pass SR 609 on right, then in 1 mile (1.6 km.) turn left downhill onto dirt road (FDR 93- sign usually missing. Note red paint blazes on trees.). In 0.2 mi. (0.3 km.) turn sharp right and in 2.7 (4.4 km.) further take right fork, FDR 371, with wildlife clearing in center of fork. Cross power line cut, then continue 3.5 mi. (5.6 km.) to turnaround and gate. Park here.

Note: FDR 93 may be closed for a week or two in early spring to avoid damage to road during spring breakup, usually late Feb. and early March. This hike may be started in Wilson's Cove, adding a few miles of driving but eliminating most of dirt roads. Follow directions for Hike #11. After parking, follow blue blazes back the way you came and begin hiking directions at 4.1 mi. (6.6 km.).

Total Travel Distance: 90 mi. (145 km.)

Trail Data

km.   mi.

0.0   0.0   From turnaround, walk straight ahead through gate on old logging road.

0.6   0.4   Vance's Cove Trail, yellow-blazed, joins from left. Follow yellow blazes for next 2.6 mi. (4.2 km.).

1.0   0.6   Va.-W.VA. state line in saddle.

4.8   3.0   Intersect Waites Run Rd. in Wilson's Cove. Turn right.

6.4   4.0   Pond Run section of Big Blue Trail, blue-blazed, goes off to left. Continue straight ahead, following blue blazes for next 4.6 mi. (7.4 km.).

6.6   4.1   Turn right onto FS road just before bridge across Waites Run. This is the County Line section of the Big Blue.

7.6   4.7   Just before crest of small ridge, trail switchbacks to right off main road and begins ascent of Great North Mountain.

10.5   6.5   Trail follows contours just below main ridge. Rocks to right of trail offer views, best when leaves are off trees.

12.2   7.6   Overlook to right, at highest point of ridge, just before trail starts to descend. If you reach flat, grassy top of ridge, go back a few hundred feet and bushwhack to rocks. With a little luck, you might even find the obscure, blue-blazed trail.

13.8 **8.6** Paul Gerhard Memorial Shelter. Leave Big Blue and, in front of shelter, turn right onto another blue-blazed trail which descends steeply.

15.0 **9.3** FDR 371; turn right.

16.3 **10.1** Parking area.

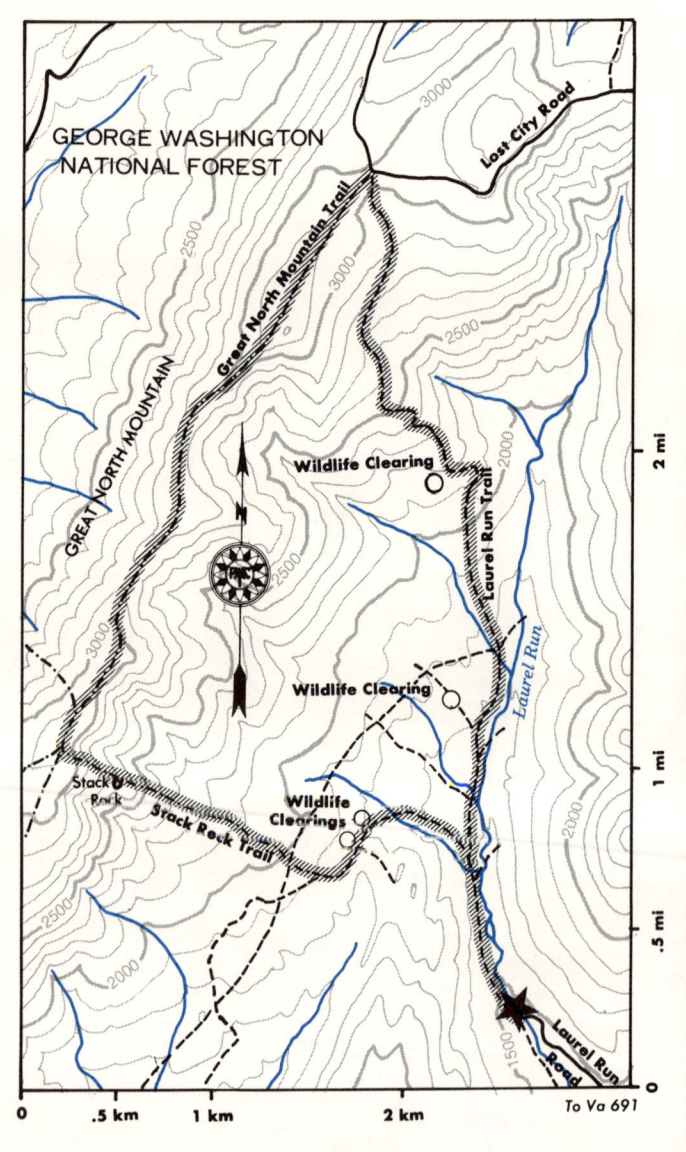

Hike No. 14

14 Laurel Run-Stack Rock
Great North Mountain, Virginia—West Virginia

Length: 8.0 mi. (12.9 km.)
Elevation Change: Approx. 1600 ft.
PATC Map F.
USGS Quads: Wolf Gap, Lost City, Va.-W.Va.

The beginning of this hike is on a logging road, passing through an area logged in 1984-1985. Towards the top of the 1600 ft. climb, the road narrows to a path which follows the rocky ridge of Great North Mountain. There are numerous opportunities for views, but the most outstanding spot is a rock outcropping just after beginning the descent on the Stack Rock Trail (sometimes known as Table Rock). From here it's all downhill to your car.

Travel Directions: I-495 to I-66; west on I-66 to I-81; south on I-81 to Va 42 marked Woodstock; south on Va 42 to Columbia Furnace (do not go toward Woodstock); right (west) onto SR 675 in Columbia Furnace; in 0.3 mi. (0.5 km.) bear left onto SR 717; in 2.5 mi. (4.0 km.) turn right onto SR 691 at Liberty Furnace; in 0.4 mi. (0.6 km.) turn left onto Forest Road 252, Laurel Run Road. Follow Laurel Run Road 1.5 mi. (2.4 km.) through private land to gate and parking lot at Laurel Run. If gate is open, you may want to drive another 0.7 mi. (1.1 km.) to foot of Stack Rock Trail, blazed purple.

Total Travel Distance: 102 mi. (164 km.)

Trail Data

km.	mi.	
0.0	**0.0**	From parking lot and gate, cross Laurel Run on culvert, following yellow-blazed road ahead. (There may be remnants of the old Laurel Run Trail following closer to the stream.)
1.1	**0.7**	Pass Stack Rock Trail coming in on left.
1.6	**1.0**	Follow yellow-blazed road straight ahead

where blue-blazed gravel road turns off to left.

5.2 3.2 Top of North Mt. ridge; intersect gravel Lost City Road; turn sharp left onto orange-blazed North Mountain Trail. Follow ridge which is Va.-W.Va. state line.

6.4 4.0 Overlook.

8.7 5.4 Stack Rock Trail, blazed purple, goes off to left. This trail may be easily passed by if you're not looking for it. It turns off just after passing through a fairly open area with a lush growth of ferns. On the right there is a weathered post with bolts in it, but the sign is gone.

9.5 5.9 Where main trail turns sharply to left, climb about 30 yards to right to Stack Rock Overlook. Return to main trail, turn right and continue descent.

11.1 6.9 Cross Laurel Run Road, blue-blazed. Continue on purple-blazed trail; skirt two wildlife clearings and descend through hollow. An old iron mine is on upper edge of first wildlife clearing, just below Laurel Run Road.

11.6 7.2 Cross rocky creek and bear right.

11.9 7.5 Laurel Run Road; follow to right, yellow-blazed.

13.2 8.2 Laurel Run, gate and parking lot.

15 Hike No. 15
Billy Goat Trail
Great Falls Park, Maryland

Length: 4.0 mi. (6.4 km.)
Elevation Change: Minimal.
PATC Map D.
USGS Quad: Falls Church, Va.

Begin this hike along the towpath of the historic Chesapeake and Ohio Canal, completed in 1850 after 22 years of work and mishap and operated for 73 years between Georgetown and Cumberland, MD. The blue-blazed Billy Goat Trail turns toward the Potomac River at Widewater (a natural wide basin where the barges were able to pass) and leads backwards in history 180 million years to the time when the palisades of the Potomac were first forming. The trail skirts the edge of Bear Island, passing giant potholes as it follows along the top of the cliffs of Mather Gorge. This portion of the hike is quite rugged and necessitates a good bit of rock scrambling. The blue blazes painted on the rocks help to locate the easiest route in most cases.

The return trip is an easy stroll along the towpath once again. Although this hike is only 4 miles (6.4 km.) in length, it may be rather slow going on the rocks—and the view will invite you to stay awhile—and enjoy! CAUTION: Use care on the rocks. Do not attempt to climb down to the water. Wear proper footgear.

Travel Directions: I-495 to Exit 15 marked Carderock and Glen Echo; take branch toward Carderock and pass Naval Ship Research and Development Center on right. At junction with MacArthur Blvd. turn left and continue west to Old Anglers Inn on right at sharp turn in road. Park in lot on left opposite the Inn.

Total Travel Distance: 3.8 mi. (6.1 km.)

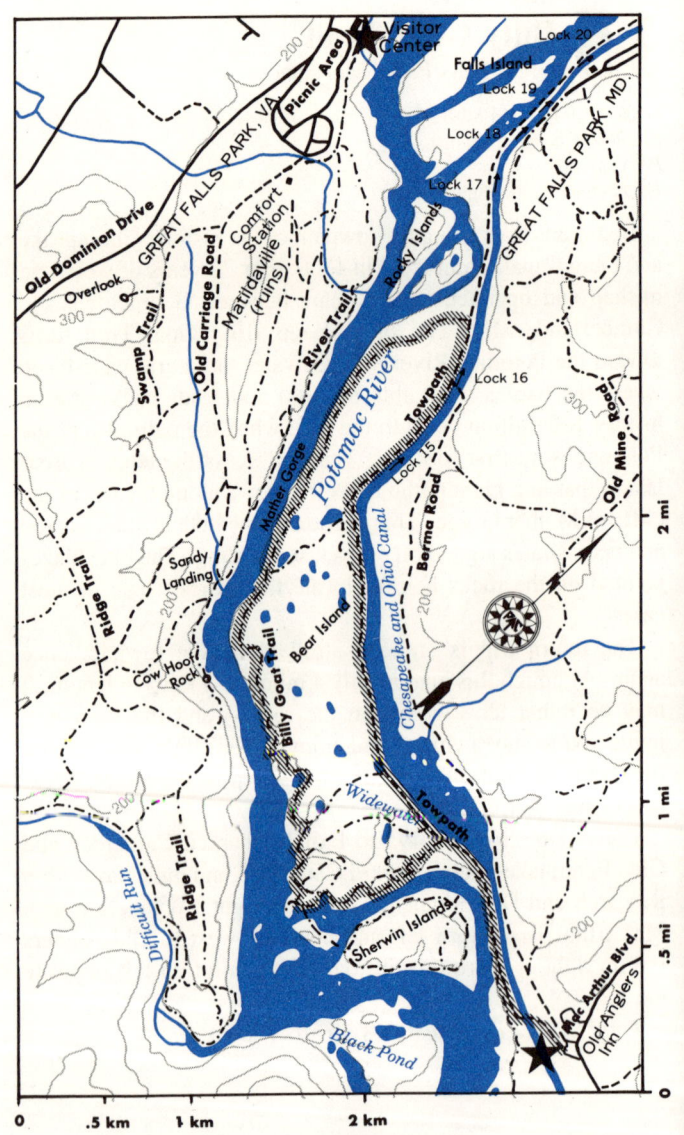

Trail Data

km.   *mi.*

0.0   **0.0**   Follow driveway to left of gate, through lower parking area; take trail to left toward canal and river.

0.2   **0.1**   C & O Canal; cross on causeway and turn right onto towpath.

0.8   **0.5**   Turn left onto blue-blazed Billy Goat Trail just after reaching Widewater; sign at trailhead. Follow blue-blazed trail until it returns to towpath.

1.0   **0.6**   Watch for trail to make short, steep descent to left between rocks. At bottom turn right.

1.5   **0.9**   Reach Potomac River; Difficult Run across river; begin travel on rocks as trail parallels river. For best route, follow blue blazes closely. Trail crosses stream, skirts to right of small pond and weaves in and out of rocks along river.

1.9   **1.2**   Rocky promontory on left, good overlook.

2.4   **1.5**   Area of giant potholes; Sandy Landing across river.

2.9   **1.8**   Veer away from Potomac slightly and travel along top of rocks above Mather Gorge; trails leading left provide better views.

3.5   **2.2**   Bear right again, leaving river, and return to towpath.

3.9   **2.4**   Reach towpath at Lock 16 and turn right. (Great Falls Park is 0.6 mi. (1.0 km.) to left.)

6.1   **3.8**   After passing Widewater, cross canal and bear right uphill to parking area.

6.4   **4.0**   Parking area.

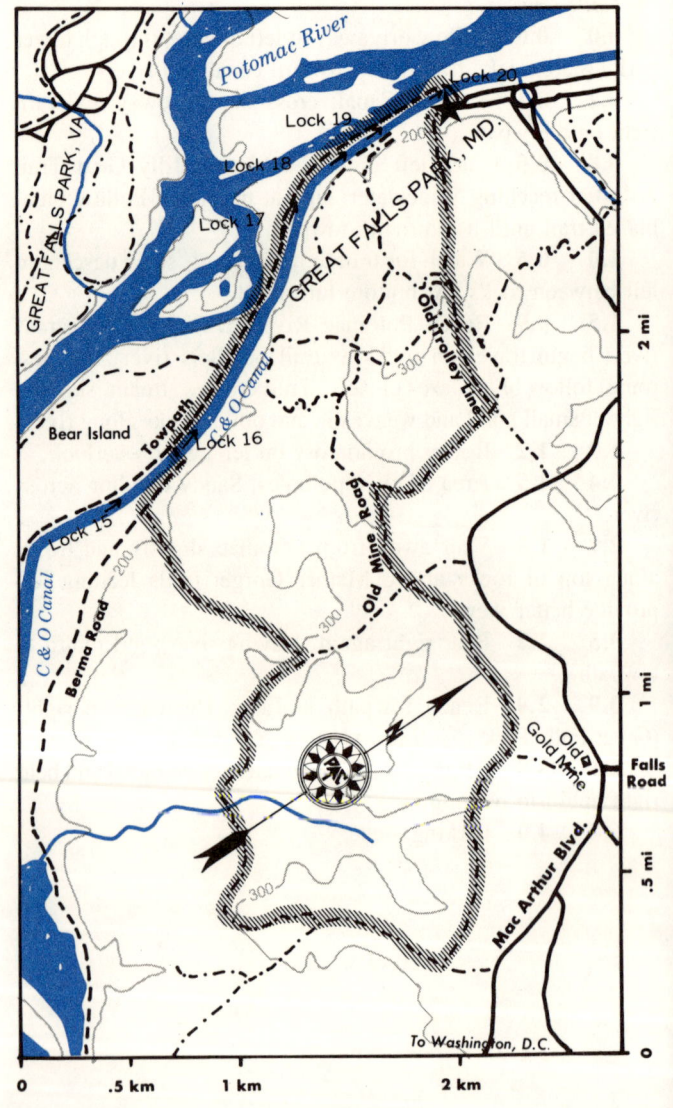

Hike No. 16
16 Great Falls
Great Falls Park, Maryland

Length: 3.5 mi. (5.6 km.)
Elevation Change: Approx. 380 ft.
PATC Map D
USGS Quad: Falls Church, Va.

This is an easy hike over mostly gentle terrain. It begins in Great Falls Park, following the towpath for about one mile (1.6 km.) before entering the woods. Watch for mounds of dirt, as much as three feet high, deposited by Appalachian mound building ants. This is also gold mining territory, dating back to the Civil War era. Remains of an abandoned gold mine lie to the right of the trail about midway in the hike. A little further along, the trail joins the bed of the old trolley line, operated from 1913 to 1921 to bring visitors from D.C. to Great Falls Park. Hike ends at Old Tavern, now a museum.

Travel Directions: I-495 to Exit 15 marked Carderock-Glen Echo; branch left towards Carderock and pass Taylor Naval Ship R and D center on right. At junction with MacArthur Blvd. turn left and continue to its end in parking lot of Great Falls Park.

Total Travel Distance: 5.6 mi. (6.1 km.)

Trail Data

km. *mi.*

0.0 **0.0** Cross canal at Lock 20 (in front of Old Tavern) and continue to left along towpath, passing Locks 19, 18 and 17.

1.0 **0.6** Recross canal on footbridge at Lock 16 and turn right onto old Berma Road. Pass lock keeper's house.

1.5 **0.9** Take yellow-blazed trail to left uphill. Look for double blaze on tree on left.

1.9 **1.2** Blue-blazed cross trail; follow it to right.

2.9 **1.8** Green-blazed trail enters from right; follow blue and green blazes to left.

3.2   **2.0**   Bear left on blue-blazed trail; green blazes lead to MacArthur Blvd.

3.7   **2.3**   Trail split; go left. Right leads to old gold mine.

4.4   **2.7**   Wide yellow-blazed trail; turn left onto it for few feet then turn right onto blue-blazed trail. Pass giant ant hills.

4.5   **2.8**   Trail split; go right, still blue-blazed.

4.8   **3.0**   Old Trolley line; bear left.

5.3   **3.3**   Trolley turnaround; go 90° and turn right down steep embankment; bear right, still on blue-blazed trail.

5.6   **3.5**   Great Falls Park and parking lot.

Hike No. 17

17 Maryland Heights-Buggy Rock
Harpers Ferry Historical Park, Maryland

Length: 4.6 mi. (7.4 km.) or 9.8 mi. (15.8 km.)
Elevation Change: Approx. 1200 ft. or 1400 ft.
PATC Map 5-6
USGS Quad: Harpers Ferry, Va.-Md.-W.Va.

History combined wth beauty! The Grant Conway Trail begins at the Potomac and climbs steadily to the ridge, passing several spectacular overlooks of the Potomac and Shenandoah Rivers, just reward for the energy expended. On the ridge are the remains of fortifications built by the Union Forces in 1862 after their defeat at Harpers Ferry. Notice the ammunition pits at several points along the trail and the remains of the main fort at the summit of Maryland Heights. The military camp was located in the level area just below the summit and here may be found scattered remains of stone tent bases, chimneys and ovens.

The circuit of 4.6 mi. (7.4 km.) can be extended to 9.8 mi. (15.8 km.) by taking a side trip along Elk Ridge. This trail is nearly level until the end where it drops about 200 ft. to Buggy Rocks, a nice lunch spot with an open view of the valley.

Travel Directions: I-495 to Va 7; west on Va 7, around Leesburg, then right onto Va 9. In about 10 miles turn right onto Va 671, then right (north) onto US 340. Cross Potomac bridge and bear right onto Va 180 to Sandy Hook Rd. Turn right onto Sandy Hook Rd., pass under bridge, then go 0.6 mi. (1.0 km.) and park in small parking area on right at foot of Grant Conway Trail.

Total Travel Distance: 46 mi. (74 km.)

Trail Data

km.	mi.	
0.0	0.0	Salmon-blazed Grant Conway Trail climbs steps from parking area. This section of trail is steep and rough.

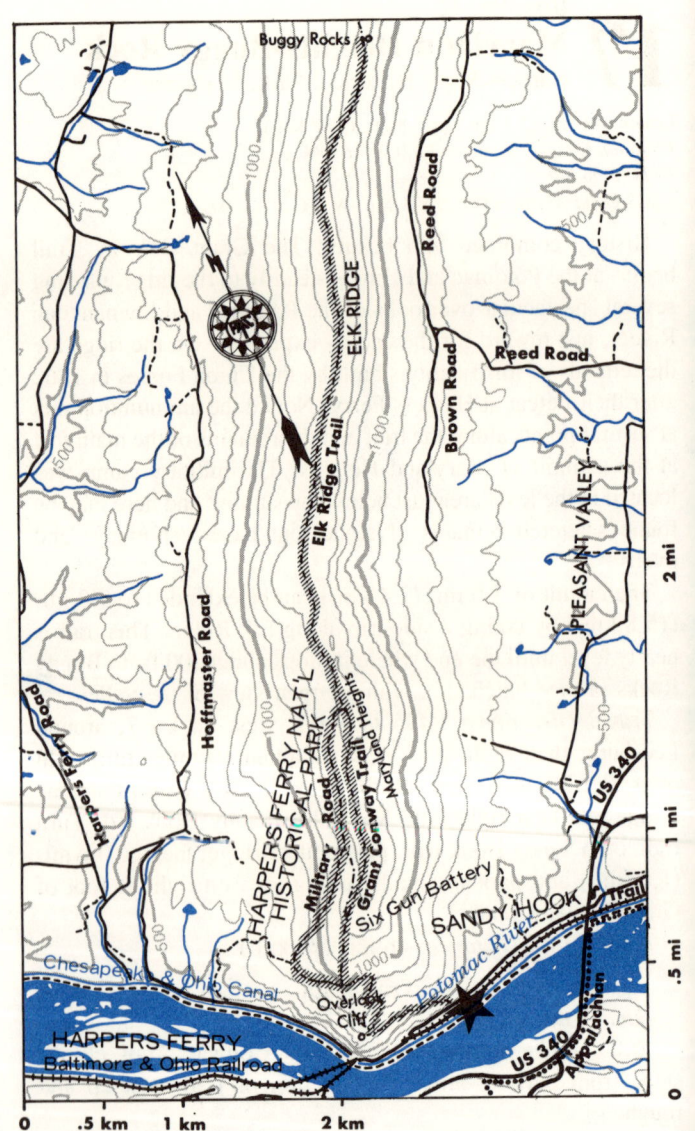

0.3 0.2 Rock outcrop-good view.
0.8 0.5 Overlook Cliff; magnificent rock formations and sweeping views of Harpers Ferry, the Potomac and the Shenandoah. Trail takes sharp right uphill from here.
1.3 0.8 At old woods road turn left.
1.5 0.9 Leave old road and take trail to right uphill, still salmon-blazed. (Straight ahead descends to Harpers Ferry Rd. and left is old trail to overlook and Naval Battery.)
1.8 1.1 Post marking "Six Gun Battery"; turn right; pass ammunition pits.
2.3 1.4 View of Pleasant Valley from rocks to right of trail.
3.2 2.0 Summit of Maryland Heights; sign to Crampton Gap. (See below for optional side trip along Elk Ridge to Buggy Rocks.) Turn left at sign, still following salmon blazes. This is location of main fort with stone ruins still visible.
3.4 2.1 Pass trail entering on right, then turn left along edge of stone fort.
4.0 2.5 Turn left onto Military Road (woods road) and descend steadily.
5.2 3.2 Leave salmon-blazed trail and follow blue-blazed trail to left uphill.
5.6 3.5 Junction with salmon-blazed trail which shortly leaves road and turns right downhill; pass overlooks; continue descent.
7.4 4.6 Parking area.

Optional Side Trip to Buggy Rocks

(This trail may become overgrow with poison ivy and briars in summer.)
0.0 0.0 At sign to Crampton Gap, follow blue-blazed trail straight ahead. Turn left along embankment, then right at trail junction. Follow nearly level ridge. Pass to east of several peaks. Pass rock overlook on right.
3.4 2.1 Bear right away from ridge and descend.

4.2   2.6   Buggy Rocks; excellent view down valley. Retrace steps to salmon-blazed Grant Conway Trail.

8.4   5.2   Cross embankment, turn right, and continue directions from 2.1 mi. (3.4 km.).

ATTENTION: There is a proposal to close the lower portion of the Grant Conway Trail to Overlook Cliff, as described at the beginning of this hike. When this happens, drive instead to the main parking area of Harpers Ferry National Historical Park. (Follow signs from US 340.) Cross the Potomac on the new Pedestrian Bridge, turn left along the C & O Canal, then cross on footbridge opposite Military Road. Begin hike here and make a side trip to Overlook Cliff. (See map.)

Hike No. 18
18 Sugar Loaf Mountain
Comus, Maryland

Length: 7.1-8.1 mi. (11.4-13.0 km.)
Elevation Change: Approx. 1400-1700 ft.
USGS Quad: Urbana, Buckeystown, Poolesville, Md.

Sugar Loaf Mountain sits like a lone sentinel to the west of I-270 just south of Frederick, Maryland. Although not particularly high as mountains go (1282 ft.), it has a summit with rugged, rocky outcroppings offering sweeping views, and miles of gentle trail winding along the slopes and foothills leading up to it.

This area, first settled in 1720, was lumbered extensively from 1785-1835 to provide charcoal for local industries. Many of the old lumber roads are still discernible and numerous charcoal hearths can be spotted along the way. Franklin D. Roosevelt was so impressed with the area that he purchased land in the Catoctin Mountains to the north, the present site of Camp David. In the 1920's Gordon Strong first began acquiring land in the area and continued buying parcels until he owned the entire mountain. Much of the hike takes place on this land, now administered by the Stronghold Foundation. The hike begins near the old carriage house, then circles into outlying areas and parts of the Monocacy Natural Resources Management Area.

Portions of the hike are on bridle trails, where pink and white slips of paper may be noticed stapled to the trees. These are route markings for the annual Arabian horse club 50 mile ride. Most of the trails are blazed and easy to follow.

The basic circuit is about 7 miles (11.3 km.) but does not go to the summit of the mountain. An additional 0.5 to 1.0 mi. (0.8-1.6 km.) to the top, as described in Options A and B, will be justly rewarded. It is a simple matter to shorten or lengthen this hike by using other combinations of trails shown on the map. The auto road leads to a parking area near the summit and

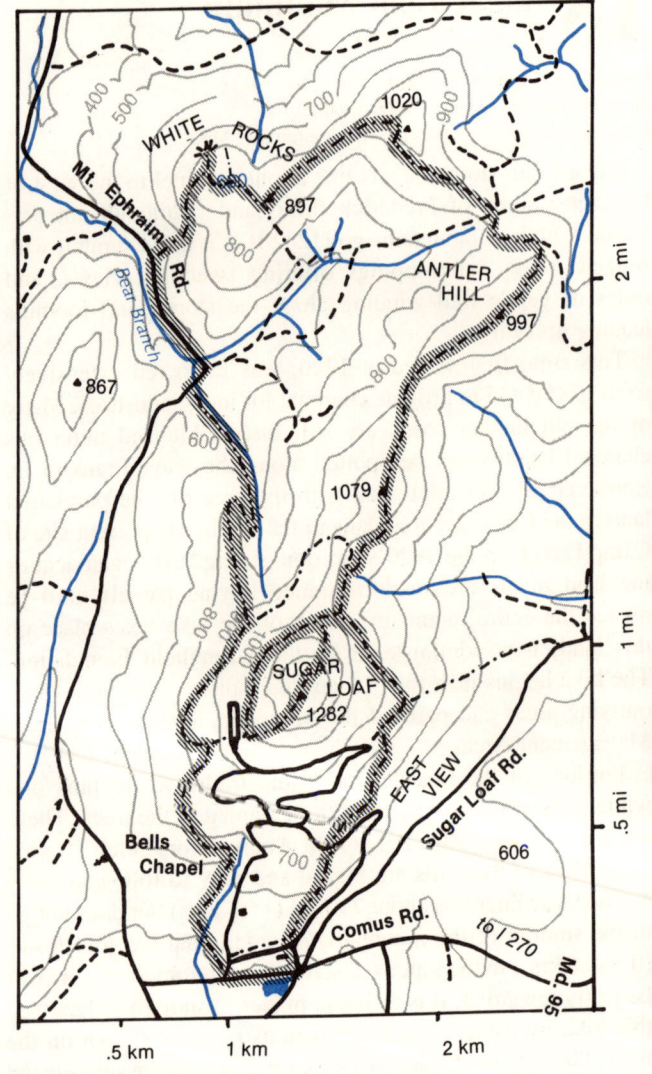

offers a good starting point for a shorter circuit.

Travel Directions: I-495 to I-270; I-270 north to Md 109 (Barnesville-Hyattstown); west on Md 109 to Comus; right on Md 95 (Comus Rd.) about 2 miles (3.2 km.) to unusual intersection of 5 roads at entrance to Stronghold Properties. Park at circle.

Total Travel Distance: 26.5 mi. (42.6 km.)

Trail Data

km. *mi.*

0.0 **0.0** Follow black-top road between concrete pillars at entrance to Stronghold Properties. Pass old carriage house on right, and just beyond take fork to left. At next road junction turn left for a few hundred feet.

0.4 **0.3** Turn right onto bridle trail, cross small stream and pass Stronghold mansions on ridge to right.

1.1 **0.7** Pass cabin, on left, built by Gordon Strong in 1920's.

1.8 **1.1** Junction with blue-blazed trail. Turn left, downhill. (To right leads 0.1 mi. (0.2 km.) to Sugar Loaf parking lot.) Continue on blue-blazed trail for next several miles.

2.5 **1.6** At double-blaze, turn left onto narrow trail and descend to stream bed.

3.0 **1.8** Turn left and follow stream.

3.7 **2.3** Turn right onto Mt. Ephraim Road (gravel), cross stream and bear left at junction with fireroad. Cross another stream.

4.2 **2.6** Turn right, steeply, uphill.

4.9 **3.1** In small clearing at top, follow trail with diamond-shaped blue blazes a few hundred feet to White Rocks Overlook with views to north. Retrace steps to clearing and turn left, downhill, following rectangular blazes. Reach cross trail and turn right. At top of hill (897 ft.) bear left and follow ridge.

6.1   **3.8**   Another summit (1029 ft.). Descend.
6.9   **4.3**   Fireroad junction. Cross and begin climb of ridge leading to main peak of Sugar Loaf.
7.3   **4.6**   Fork in trail; bear right. At top of ridge is winter only view of ridge just traversed.
7.6   **4.7**   Top of Antler Hill (997 ft.).
7.7   **4.8**   Rattlesnake Rocks.
8.0   **5.0**   Second summit of Antler Hill with views west and northwest.
8.5   **5.3**   Summit (1079 ft.).
9.2   **5.7**   Junction with horse trail. Turn left.
9.3   **5.8**   Trail junction. For shorter hike, go left on white-blazed horse trail with wooden arrow on tree. For slightly longer hike via summit (definitely worth the trip) take Option A or B.

Option A: Turn right on blue and white-blazed trail, short distance to red-blazed trail. Follow red blazes left to summit and return via same route. (Approx. 0.5 mi. or 0.8 km. total)

Option B: Same as above to summit. From summit descend, via yellow-blazed trail and stone steps, to parking lot for auto road. Turn right, pass concession stand and immediately take blue and white-blazed trail to right around base of summit to junction with red-blazed trail. Continue straight on blue and white-blazed trail to junction. (Approx. 1.0 mi. or 1.6 km. total) To continue hike, follow white-blazed horse trail and wooden arrow on tree.

10.0   **6.2**   Turn left and descend on narrow horse trail, marked by arrow on tree to right of junction. White blazes lead a short distance to Sugar Loaf East View picnic area and parking lot.
10.8   **6.7**   Cross auto road.
11.1   **6.9**   Turn right onto hard-surfaced road and pass to left of carriage house.
11.4   **7.1**   Parking area.

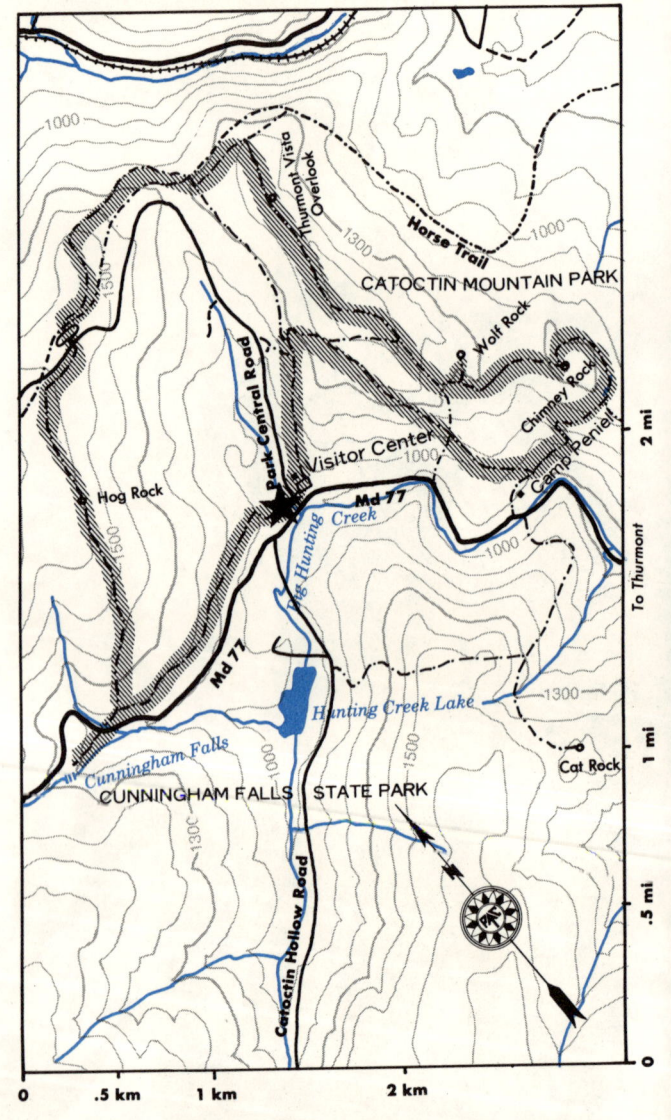

Hike No. 19

19 Wolf-Chimney Rocks
Catoctin Mountain Park, Thurmont, Maryland

Length: 8.7 mi. (14.0 km.)
Elevation Change: Approx. 1200 ft.
Sketch map available at Visitor Center.
USGS Quad: Blue Ridge Summit, Md.

The trails for this hike are located within the boundaries of Catoctin Mountain Park with the exception of a side trail leading to Cunningham Falls in the state park of that name. They are wide and well maintained but rocky in some parts.

Most of this area was clear cut in the 1800's for making charcoal to fuel nearby Catoctin Iron Furnace. The beginning of the hike is a self-guiding nature trail, followed by a side trip to Cunningham Falls. Although most of the hiking will be through deciduous woods, this area changes abruptly to evergreen upon crossing the road to the falls.

From the falls the trail returns to Catoctin Park and climbs the ridge for the first in a series of rocky overlooks. Hog Rock takes its name from the days of the early settlers whose hogs would gather there to eat nuts in the fall. Since this was the ideal time for slaughter it was very convenient for the farmers to go there to catch their fattened pigs. The next overlook is Thurmont Vista with a view of the town of Thurmont, then Wolf Rock, named for a rock formation resembling a wolf's head and Chimney Rock with its rock chimney. The greenish rock formations at Cunningham Falls and along Hog Rock Trail are Catoctin Greenstone while those at Wolf and Chimney Rocks are Weverton Quartzite.

This hike may be combined with the Cat Rock hike for a slightly longer trip. See below.

Travel Directions: I-495 to I-270; I-270 north to US 15 near Frederick, Md; US 15 north to Md 77 near Thurmont; Md 77 west about 3 miles (4.8 km.) to Catoctin Mountain Park Visitor Center on right.

Total Travel Distance: 52 mi. (84 km.)

Trail Data

km. mi.

0.0 **0.0** Park in lot to left of Visitor Center. Follow sign to Cunningham Falls.

1.9 **1.2** Trail junction and sign for Cunningham Falls; turn left and cross road to falls.

2.3 **1.4** Cunningham Falls; retrace steps across road and continue past sign for Cunningham Falls and Hog Rock.

4.2 **2.6** Hog Rock Overlook, elevation 1620 ft.

5.0 **3.1** Cross Park Central Road and continue through picnic area; pass trail on right and shortly curve to right on well worn path.

6.6 **4.1** Wide cross trail; turn left.

6.9 **4.3** Fork in trail; bear right.

7.2 **4.5** Thurmont Vista Overlook.

8.5 **5.3** Trail junction; continue straight ahead to Wolf Rock. Trail to right goes to Park Headquarters.

9.0 **5.6** Wolf Rock. (*Caution:* There are very deep crevices both here and at Chimney Rocks.) Return to main trail and turn left.

9.8 **6.1** Sign to Park Headquarters; continue straight ahead to Chimney Rocks with excellent view. Cat Rock is visible on ridge directly opposite. Return to main trail and turn right (sign to Park Headquarters). (See below for shorter return route from here, alternate C.)

10.5 **6.5** Sign for Park Headquarters and Crow's Nest (campground); turn right.

11.3 **7.0** Take right trail to Park Central Road. Left trail goes to Park Headquarters. (See below for alternate return routes, one shorter, one longer.) Ascend ridge and pass turnoff to Wolf Rock.

13.2 **8.2** Trail junction; follow signs to Visitor Center.

14.0 **8.7** Visitor Center.

Alternate return routes:

(A) Continue straight ahead and cross road to Cat Rock parking area. See directions for *Cat Rock Hike*-No. 20.

(B) For a shorter return which eliminates the climb required on other two trails, continue straight ahead to road and turn right about a mile to Visitor Center. Either walk along the road or cross the road and follow fishermen's paths along the stream paralleling the road.

(C) This route requires a little backtracking, but it is considerably shorter and involves less climbing. From Chimney Rocks, retrace steps to Wolf Rock. At sign bear left toward Park Headquarters. At next intersection and sign to Wolf Rock, turn right and continue down hill. Turn left at next intersection, following sign to Visitor Center.

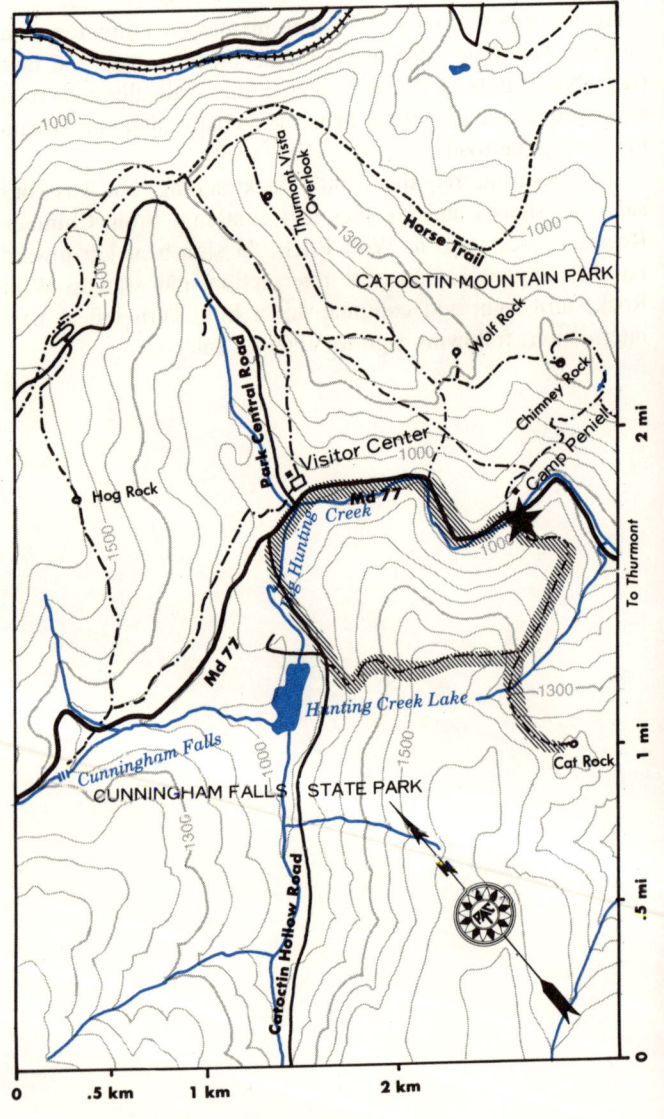

Hike No. 20
20 Cat Rock
Cunningham Falls State Park,
Thurmont, Maryland

Length: 4.4 mi. (7.1 km.)
Elevation Change: Approx. 560 ft.
Sketch map available at park Visitor Center.
USGS Quads: Blue Ridge Summit, Catoctin Furnace, Md.

A climb of about one mile (1.6 km.) on a well graded footpath will bring you to 3 outcroppings of rock typical of that found along the crest of the Catoctin ridge and known as Weverton Quartzite. The first mass of rocks is immediately to the right of the main trail and appears from below as a sparkling white dome glistening in the sun. If you enjoy a little rock scrambling, the view from the top is worth the effort. Two other overlooks are slightly off the trail to the north and south. From here the trail travels along the ridge before beginning a steep descent to Hunting Creek Lake and a walk along the road to the parking lot.

This hike can be started from the Visitor Center, or combined with Hike No. 19, making a circuit of 10.5 mi. (17 km.).

Travel Directions: I-495 to I-270; north on I-270 to US 15 outside Fredrick; north on US 15 to Md 77 at Thurmont; west on Md 77 about 2 miles (3.2 km.) to parking lot on left, across from Administrative Offices.

Total Travel Distance: 50 mi. (82 km.)

Trail Data

km.	mi.	
0.0	0.0	Well worn trail to Cat Rock angles to left and uphill as you enter parking lot.
1.5	0.9	Sign and trail leading right to lake; bear left. (This is the trail you will return to after visiting the rocks.)
1.9	1.2	Cat Rock; main overlook immediately to right of trail; north overlook and south overlook few hundred feet on side trails.

2.4 1.5 Retrace steps to trail leading left to lake. (Lush growth of ferns here.)

3.1 1.9 Partial overlook from edge of ridge.

3.7 2.3 Begin steep descent to lake.

4.4 2.7 Reach Hunting Creek Lake; turn right onto Catoctin Hollow Road.

5.2 3.2 Little Hunting Creek. Do not cross. Descend embankment to right and follow fishermen's paths along stream bank to parking lot. (*Alternate route:* Continue on Catoctin Hollow Road another 200-300 feet to Md 77 and turn right, passing Visitor Center and on to parking lot.)

7.1 4.4 Parking lot.

Hike No. 21
21 Caledonia-Quarry Gap
Michaux State Forest, Pennsylvania

Length: 7.4 mi. (11.9 km.)
Elevation Change: Approx. 820 ft.
PATC Map 2-3.
USGS Quad: Caledonia Park, Pa.

This "figure-eight" hike begins in Caledonia State Park, site of an iron works erected in 1837 and burned during the Civil War. The first part follows the Old Rolling Mill Race lined with rhododendron, huge pines and hemlocks, then climbs to the top of Ore Bank Hill where it joins the Appalachian Trail. After a short distance the Locust Gap Trail is reached and followed downhill to the Hosack Run Trail which climbs along the stream through the narrow, rocky gorge known as "Dark Hollow" with more rhododendron, pines and hemlocks. The return is on the Appalachian Trail which passes the Quarry Gap shelters then descends to Caledonia Park.

Travel Directions: I-495 to I-270; I-270 north to US 15 outside Frederick; north on US 15 to US 30 near Gettysburg; west on US 30 About 18 miles (29 km.) to Pa 233; north on Pa 233 and immediately turn left. Pass park office and road leading right uphill to camping area. Park in first lot on left.

Total Travel Distance: 87 mi. (140 km.)

Trail Data

km.   *mi.*

0.0   0.0   From parking lot walk south (toward US 30), along right side of large grassy area, crossing stream on footbridge. Turn right onto Ramble Trail, yellow-blazed, and follow along south bank of stream.

1.1   0.7   Cross stream on bridge and bear right, crossing several branches. (This is a slight backtrack but a lovely walk. For a more direct route, after leaving parking lot, do not cross stream; instead turn right on Ramble Trail and walk

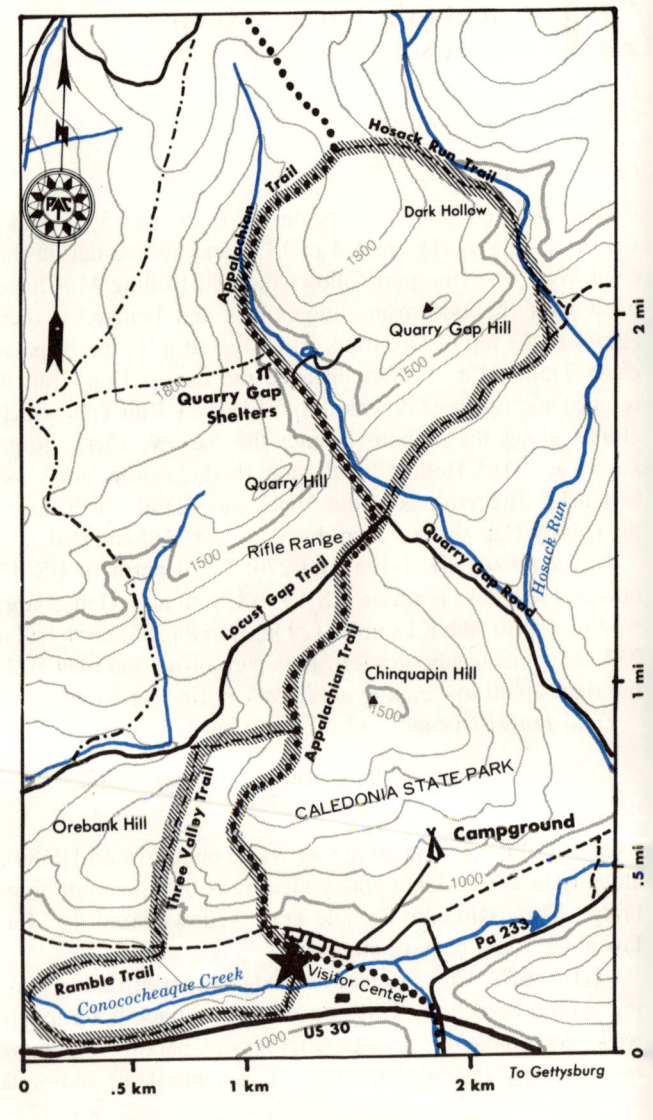

along north bank of stream to turnoff, right, as described below.)

1.8 **1.1** Turn left onto wide, blue-blazed trail. At this spot there is a large tree and a bench in the intersection where yellow trail goes right and blue trail branches left.

2.3 **1.4** Cross trail; bear right, still blue-blazed.

2.6 **1.6** Meet white-blazed Appalachian Trail; turn left.

3.7 **2.3** Locust Gap Trail, blue-blazed, actually a dirt road with rifle range on far side; turn right.

3.9 **2.4** Appalachian Trail goes left; continue straight ahead on road.

4.2 **2.6** Quarry Gap Road bends sharp right downhill. Bear left from small clearing on left and continue on blue-blazed Locust Gap Trail. Cross stream twice.

6.1 **3.8** Trail split in clearing *before* crossing stream. Leave Locust Gap Trail and bear left on Hosack Run Trail, crossing stream twice as you climb through Dark Hollow.

7.6 **4.7** Sharp left and steep ascent leaving gorge, still blue-blazed.

8.1 **5.0** Reach Appalachian Trail, white-blazed, and turn left. (The rest of the hike will be along the Appalachian Trail.)

9.2 **5.7** Pass Quarry Gap shelters on right; good water.

10.0 **6.2** Meet Locust Gap Trail (dirt road); turn right.

10.1 **6.3** Leave dirt road and continue on white-blazed AT to left.

11.3 **7.0** Fork in trail; go left. Descend steeply.

11.9 **7.4** Cross water line cut and continue straight to parking lot.

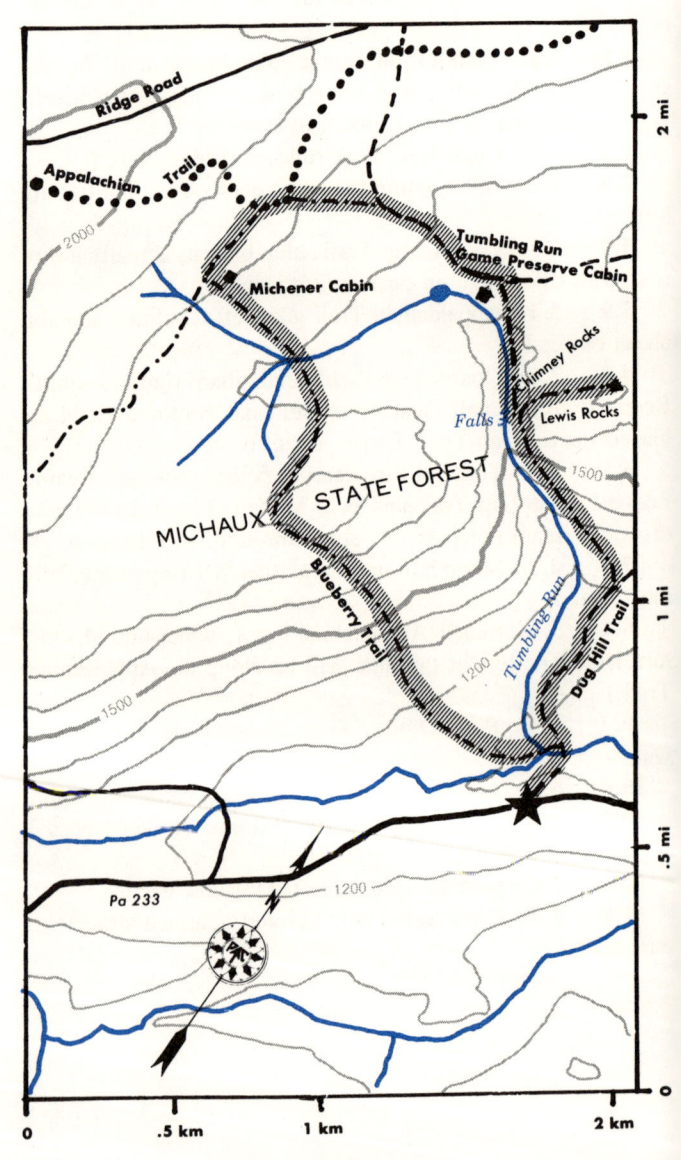

Hike No. 22
22 Tumbling Run-Lewis Rocks
Michaux State Forest, Pennsylvania

Length: 5.0 mi. (8.1 km.)
Elevation Change: Approx. 760 ft.
PATC Map 2-3.
USGS Quad: Dickinson, Walnut Bottom, Pa.

Climb steeply along Tumbling Run, a rocky streambed very appropriately named, until you reach a waterfall, then strike out to the right and climb onto a large rock outcropping known as Chimney Rocks. The rocks are interesting but the view not far reaching. Further along the ridge to the northeast are Lewis Rocks, offering a spectacular view from the top and a cave beneath where Lewis the Robber is said to have hidden his treasure in the 1800's.

Next the trail passes the Tumbling Run Game Preserve Cabin, privately owned as is most of the land along Tumbling Run. Hikers are welcome to use the trail so long as they do not litter, build fires or camp. The folks who own this cabin take great pride in it and spend a lot of time keeping it neat and in good repair. After a short stretch of the Appalachian Trail the route passes Michener Cabin (a PATC locked cabin, rented through PATC Headquarters). Here are several springs feeding into a white, sandy-bottomed stream. Leaving the cabin area, the Blueberry Trail passes through an area of tall trees with a dense blanket of blueberry bushes beneath. Continue downhill to car.

This hike is not long in miles but offers much opportunity for exploring and savoring.

Travel Directions: I-495 to I-270; I-270 to US 15 near Frederick; US 15 north to US 30; US 30 west through Gettysburg to Pa 233; Pa 233 north about 9.6 mi. (15.5 km.) to Cumberland County line. (Watch for sign on post on right. Park in pulloff on left).

Total Travel Distance: 101 mi. (162 km.)

Trail Data

km.   *mi.*

0.0   **0.0**   Follow Old Dughill Road, an old dirt road leading from parking area.

0.2   **0.1**   Stream and washed out bridge; swing left, cross stream, then bear right back to Old Dughill Road and turn left. (Do not take blue-blazed trail.)

0.5   **0.3**   Old Dughill Road forks to right. Follow trail straight ahead which leads to edge of Tumbling Run. Climb steadily along right bank.

1.4   **0.9**   Waterfalls; continue steep ascent to level open area; bear right away from stream toward rock formations; there are many paths, take your pick. (To avoid some of the rock scrambling, begin climbing to right from base of large falls.)

1.6   **1.0**   Chimney Rocks–explore these then walk slightly uphill in NE direction and follow ridge, passing several outcroppings, to highest point.

2.1   **1.3**   Highest point of rocks, Lewis Rocks; scramble to top for view; cave is in rocks to north. Retrace steps along ridge to Chimney Rocks. Just before reaching Chimney Rocks, look for a narrow path forking back to your right. Turn right onto this trail which leads back in direction of Lewis Rocks, but this time veering off to left of them.

3.1   **1.9**   Reach old road and turn left.

3.2   **2.0**   Game Preserve cabin, private property. Pass to right of cabin and follow access road. (Do not take path near lake.)

4.2   **2.6**   Turn left onto white-blazed Appalachian Trail.

4.8   **3.0**   Leave AT and take wide, blue-blazed trail leading sharp left to Michener Cabin.

5.1   **3.3**   Michener Cabin; follow blue-blazed Blueberry Hill Trail from front of cabin.

6.3   **4.0**   Cross rock ledges; partial view.
7.7   **4.9**   Reach Tumbling Run; leave blue blazes, cross stream to right and bear left on old road to Old Dughill Road.
7.9   **5.0**   Parking area.

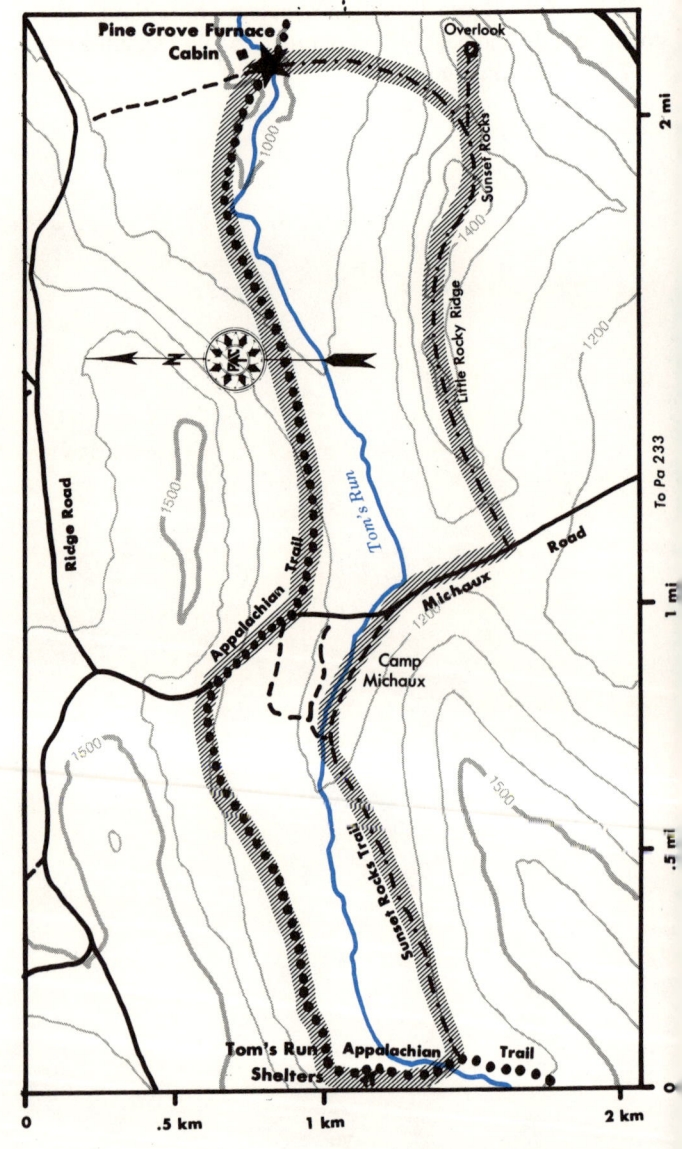

Hike No. 23
23 Sunset Rocks
Michaux State Forst, Pennsylvania

Length: 4.8 mi. (7.7 km.)
Elevation Change: Approx. 800 ft.
PATC Map 2-3.
USGS Quad: Dickinson, Pa.

This hike begins at the site of 150 year old Pine Grove Furnace Cabin (scheduled for removal), just before crossing Tom's Run. A little further on the trail enters open fields and passes the ruins of buildings in an area known as Camp Michaux. This was originally a farm and was made into a CCC camp in the 1930's. During World War II it served as a prisoner of war camp where many high ranking German officers were held. After the war it became a church camp and was finally abandoned in 1975. The imposing stone ruin was the scene of an Indian raid and massacre.

This section of trail is part of the Appalachian Trail and continues over easy terrain to the Tom's Run shelters. At the shelters the Sunset Rocks Trail branches off, passes through an area logged in 1984 after gypsy moth damage, then leads steeply to the ridge crest and the backbone of rocks known as Sunset Rocks. There follows nearly a mile of very rough trail and rock scrambling with some views and some interesting rock formations for those who like to climb a little higher. At the end of the ridge is an overlook, just before descending to the starting point at Tom's Run.

Travel Directions: I-495 to I-270; I-270 north to US 15 near Frederick, Md; US 15 north to US 30; US 30 west through Gettysburg to Pa 233; Pa 233 north to Pine Grove Furnace. Just before Park Headquarters on right, turn left onto narrow dirt road going uphill. Join white blazes of Appalachian Trail and park below Pine Grove Furnace Cabin site, before crossing Tom's Run.

Total Travel Distance: 105 mi. (169 km.)

Trail Data

km.   mi.

0.0   0.0   Cross stream on footbridge and follow white-blazed AT on dirt road below cabin site.

1.1   0.7   Leave road and branch to right on grassy road, passing old foundations.

1.5   0.9   Pass Camp Michaux and rejoin hard-surfaced road; go right.

1.6   1.0   Turn left off road, still on white-blazed AT.

3.5   2.2   Tom's Run shelters; cross stream and just beyond take blue-blazed Sunset Rocks Trail to left. Pass through area of logging. Trail joins logging road, then goes off to right, skirting to right of clearing. It follows line of trees on right, parallel to road.

5.5   3.4   Michaux Road; turn right then left into woods, following blue blazes; ascend to ridge.

6.3   3.9   Reach crest of ridge and bear left along Sunset Rocks.

6.9   4.3   Blue-blazed trail leading steeply downhill to left completes circuit. Overlook is straight ahead about 300 ft., also blue-blazed.

7.8   4.7   Parking area.

Hike No. 24
24 Pole Steeple
Michaux State Forest, Pennsylvania

Length: 6.3 mi. (10.1 km.)
Elevation Change: Approx. 480 ft.
PATC Map 2-3.
USGS Quad: Dickinson, Pa.

The Pole Steeple hike begins in Pine Grove Furnace State Park, a park developed around the site of an iron furnace which was active from 1765 to the 1880's, the stack of which is still standing near the parking lot behind the park office. The trail first passes Fuller Lake, the old ore hole from which the iron was mined, and which now serves as a public bathing beach from Memorial Day to Labor Day. The Appalachian Trail is followed next, then Old Forge Road, now overgrown and not much more than a good mountain trail. A short side trail climbs steeply to Pole Steeple, a rugged quartzite cliff named many years ago by boy scouts who erected a flag pole there. The cliffs overlook Laurel Lake, created when Mountain Valley Creek was dammed to provide power for the forge hammer. A gradual descent can be made by returning to Old Forge Road, or a steeper one by following the blue blazes between the rocks and passing below them. The circuit is completed by walking a section of the old railroad bed, now a road, passing Laurel Lake and returning to the park.

Travel Directions: I-495 to I-270; I-270 north to US 15 near Frederick, Md; US 15 north to US 30; US 30 west through Gettysburg to Pa 233; Pa 233 north to Pine Grove Furnace State Park. At fork bear right, leaving Pa 233. Pass Park Headquarters on right and park in lot marked Fuller Lake Recreation Area.

Total Travel Distance: 105 mi. (169 km.)

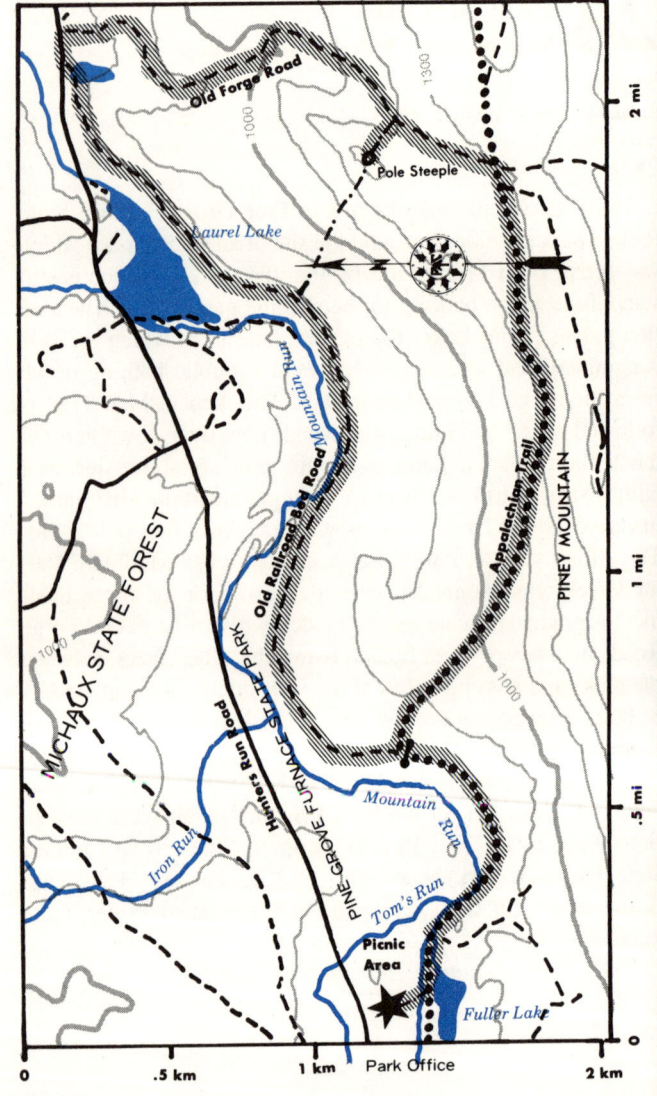

Trail Data

km.   mi.

0.0   0.0   Walk to far end of parking lot, pass comfort station and take trail leading across footbridge to lake. Turn left and follow shoreline of Fuller Lake. At end of lake locate white blazes of Appalachian Trail (double blaze on bridge post) and follow them as they bear to the right.

1.1   0.7   Gate; follow white AT blazes uphill to the right; ascend north slope of Piney Mountain.

1.5   0.9   Pass to right of landfill.

3.4   2.1   Road enters on right; continue straight ahead.

3.5   2.2   Leave AT and turn left onto blue-blazed Old Forge Road.

4.0   2.5   Just before double blaze on tree, turn left and ascend steeply to Pole Steeple.

4.5   2.8   Pole Steeple; enjoy the view then return to Old Forge Road and turn left (unblazed). For alternate route see below.

5.2   3.2   Pass cabin; bear left.

5.6   3.5   Reach hardtop road; turn sharp left onto old railroad bed, now a road.

9.0   5.6   AT joins trail from left; continue straight ahead past gate.

10.1   6.3   Parking area.

Alternate return route from rocks: From Pole Steeple follow blue blazes down the rock slide in the center of the rocks—or skirt the entire cliff to the left and rejoin the blue blazes at the base. Follow this blue-blazed trail about 0.5 mi. (0.8 km.) to the road and turn left to the parking area, as in the above directions.

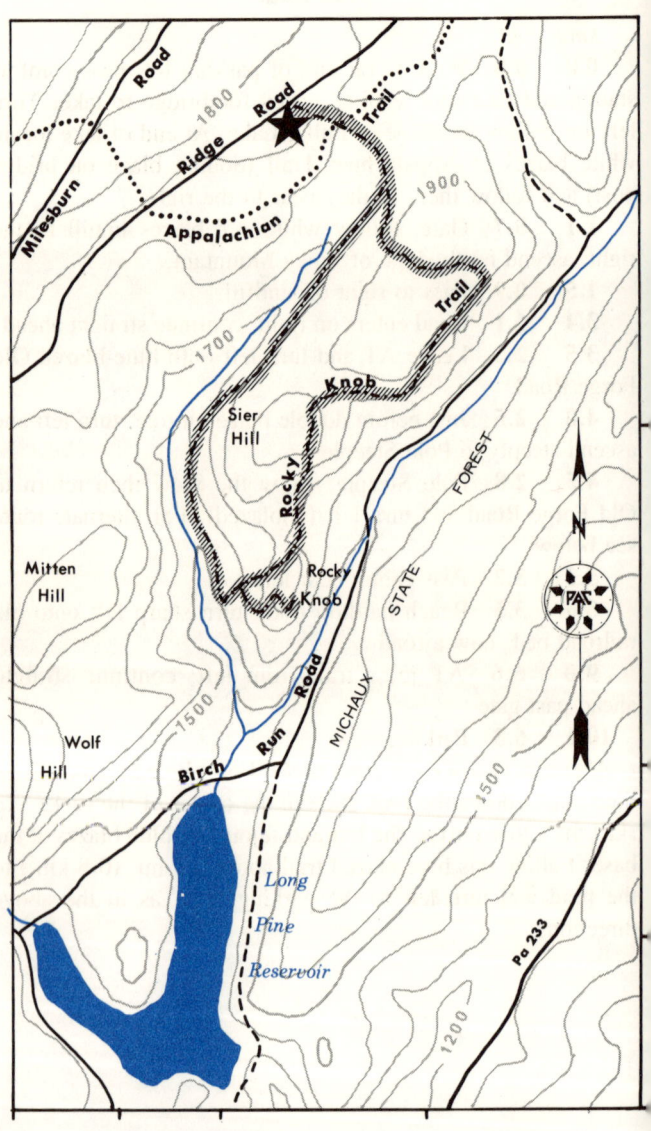

Hike No. 25
25 Rocky Knob
Michaux State Forest, Pennsylvania

Length: 4.2 mi. (6.8 km.)
Elevation Change: Approx. 800 ft.
Brochure available at Caledonia State Park.
USGS Quad: Caledonia Park, Pa.

The Rocky Knob Trail is a gentle, ridgetop walk, with some outstanding views and a short scramble to the top of Rocky Knob. The walk begins on an old section of road built by the CCC in 1937, but never completed because of the rugged geology of the area. In 1976 the YCC (Youth Conservation Corps) constructed the current loop trail and the following summer added the numbered stations making it an interpretative trail. (Map and information courtesy of Pennsylvania Bureau of Forestry and YCC.)

Travel Directions: I-495 to I-270; I-270 north to US 15 at Frederick; north on US 15 to US 30 near Gettysburg; west on US 30 through Gettysburg about 18 miles (29 km.) to Pa 233; north on Pa 233 1.5 mi. (2.4 km.) then turn left onto Milesburn Road. In 2.9 mi. (4.7 km.) take right fork and in another 1.4 mi. (2.3 km.) take sharp right onto Ridge Road toward Mt. Holly Drive 1.6 mi. (2.6 km.) to trailhead on right with sign and pulloff area.

Total Travel Distance: 96 mi. (154.5 km.)

Trail Data

km.   mi.

0.0   0.0   Ridge Rd.; Follow old roadbed; entire trail marked by green Keystone blazes. Cross white-blazed Appalachian Trail.

0.6   0.4   (Station # 2) Stunted forest growth is a result of poor sandy and rocky soil.

1.0   0.6   (Station # 4) Allegheny mound-building ants. Please do not distrub.

1.1 **0.7** (Station # 5) Although small in size, the trees in this area are over 40 years old, their stunted condition caused by poor soil, repeated fires and overbrowsing by deer.

1.3 **0.8** (Station # 6) Looking eastward is East Big Flat Ridge; Pa 233 is in the next valley.

1.9 **1.2** (Station # 9) Sier Hill; Long Pine dam below, with Rocky Knob, Wolf's Hill and Mitten Hill to the right.

3.4 **2.1** (Station #11) A side trail leads over rocks to the flat summit of Rocky Knob.

3.7 **2.3** (Station #12) Top of Rocky Knob; Long Pine Reservoir directly below. Return to Station #11 and continue downhill to left.

4.2 **2.6** (Station #13) Trail returns to old roadbed and turns right.

6.3 **3.9** End of loop; continue straight.

6.8 **4.2** Ridge Road.